ISBN-10 0-929061-04-7
ISBN-13 978-0-929061-04-7

MW01120090

序言

根據交通部的統計，每年取得駕駛執照的人數約有二十五萬人，為了提高新牌駕駛者的技術，及改善以往持新牌人仕容易發生意外的記錄，分級考牌制度(Graduated Licensing)已於一九九四年四月一日全面實施。

簡單來説，分級考牌制度也即「二級制」過兩關路試，第一路試考牌約二十分鐘，務求考牌者駕駛控制能力自如，平行泊車、三點式掉頭、上落山停車、泊位等技術一定要練習純熟安全。第二路試，考牌約四十分鐘，要求較嚴格，將考驗考生所有應懂的駕駛技術，如第一次路試內容及加上高速公路駕駛、路邊停車、小路左轉到繁忙大街。如有良好的技術和信心，在路上練習的時間足夠，一定成功過關。

在安大略省必須年滿十六歲才可考駕駛執照，一般新學者都要先考 G 牌(即私家車，客貨車及小型貨車)，日後如要考專業 A to F 牌照，請到交通部查詢。旅遊人仕如有國際車牌才可以在安省駕駛。

新安大略省居民，如果持有其他國家的有效駕駛執照，六十日內繼續使用該駕駛執照，六十日後應考取安省執照。

如持有美國、日本、韓國、德國、法國、英國、奧地利、比利時、瑞士、加拿大其他省份或區域有效駕駛執照，兩年或以上者，到牌照部驗眼及交費用即可發出安省駕駛執照(Exchange Agreement)，如在兩年以下即排期考 G 路試，如不及格也可得到G2牌在安省繼續駕駛。

如果來自其他國家，如香港、東南亞、中國、中美洲、歐洲等國，沒有交換協議者(No Exchange Agreement)，安省駕駛廳會依照駕駛者持有的有效日期來制定：

1.如果在兩年以上者，即可排期考 G 或 G2 路試
2.如果在兩年以下至十二個月牌者，即可排期考 G2 路試
3.如果在十二個月以下至一個月的牌照要依安省的等候時間加減才可排期考 G2 路試

詳情請到考牌部查詢。

本書以最精簡編寫，內容分兩部份，「筆試」及「路試」，圖文並茂，同時獲得運輸署提供最新資料，令本書更充實詳盡，特此鳴謝。筆者很高興能向安省政府提議中文筆試成功，幫助數十萬華人通過中文筆試，獲得車牌，並不斷提倡安全駕駛。應知好的駕駛習慣和技術，人人有責任，除了保障路上駕駛者，還保障你、你的家人，達到安全駕駛的理想！

"Part of the information contained herein is from the Ontario Ministry of Transportation and Driver's Handbook. Reprinted with permission of the Ministry of Transportation."

法律顧問： 何志立律師
Legal Consultant: Sunny C. Ho

編者

梁成基
TOM LEUNG

目錄
Table of Content

1. 序言 P.1
2. 多倫多5個考中英文筆試及路試地址 P.3
3. 安省分級考牌制度 P.4
4. 筆試過程及機器用法 P.5

第一部份：筆試

5. 交通符號 .... P.7 - P.15
6. 駕駛常識 .... P.16 - P.50
7. 安省駕駛執照制度 P.51

第二部份：路試

8. 自動波 P.53
9. 交叉手正確方法 P.53
10. 正確停車位置 P.54
11. 盲點及換線方法 P.55
12. 馬路行車線 P.56
13. 保持兩秒鐘跟車距離方法 P.57
14. 日間與夜間駕駛 P.58
15. 左轉及右轉的重點 P.59
16. 三點式掉頭 P.60
17. 斜坡泊車方法 P.60
18. 平行泊車 P.61
19. 九十度角前後泊車法 P.62
20. 史密夫駕駛方法 P.63
21. 交通燈號 P.64
22. 單程路 P.66
23. 什麼是防禦駕駛? P.67
24. 高速公路駕駛方法 P.69
25. 路邊停車 P.71
26. 汽車意外應如何處理 P.72
27. 多倫多市交通意外報案中心 P.73
28. 冬天駕駛須知 P.74
29. 怎樣考路試成功? P.76
30. 東區考試場貼士 P.77
31. 汽車保養 P.80
32. 廿十點節省汽油的方法 P.82
33. 購買新車舊車須知 P.83
34. 常見交通符號 P.84
35. 路試常用英語 P.85
36. 駕駛過失點扣分表 P.87

© 2008 Budget Publishing Co. 版權所有 不得翻印
ISBN-10 0-929061-04-7
ISBN-13 978-0-929061-04-7

多倫多5個考中英文筆試及路試地址
5 Locations Driving Test Exam Centre: Written & Road Test

1. 777 Bay St. (at College St.)
(at TD Bank Lower level)
在道明銀行下面 (只有筆試)
8:30 am – 5:00 pm (Mon – Fri)

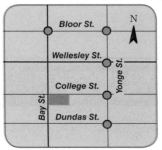

2. 1448 Lawrence Avenue East
(at Victoria Park Avenue)
8:30 am – 5:00 pm (Mon – Fri)

● SUBWAY
STATION
地底車站

3. 37 Carl Hall Road
(Sheppard Ave. W. & Keele St.)
8:30 am – 5:00 pm (Mon – Fri)

4. 65 Grand Marshall Dr.
(Sheppard Ave. E. & Morningside Ave.)
9:00 am – 5:00 pm (Mon – Sat)

5. 5555 Eglinton Ave. West
Etobicoke
8:30 am – 5:00 pm (Mon – Fri)

Tel: **(416) 325-8580** or **1-888-570-6110**
www.drivetest.ca

Outside Toronto 多倫多市外

6. 1 Henderson Dr. (AURORA)
Tel: (905) 713-6941

7. 59 First Gulf Blvd. Unit 9 (BRAMPTON)
Tel: (905) 793-4340

8. 200 John St. W. (at Park Rd.) (OSHAWA)
Tel: 1(905) 728-7789

Road Test Appointment 路試預約電話

416-325-8580 & 1-888-570-6110

考筆試前要注意事項：

1. 費用：$125 (G1)
2. 視力不足，請帶同眼鏡
3. 請帶同能證明身份的證件
   如：護照、出世紙、
   公民證、移民入境紙
   (如有工作證可一同帶去)
4. 請帶同原居地駕駛執照

3

安省分級考牌制度

Graduated Licensing Program of Ontario

安省新制度「分級考牌」經過多年來提議，考慮計劃終於在一九九四年四月一日，正式實施。

如在四月一日前考到筆試者要在六月六日前考到路試否則撥入新例，新例分為兩階段簡稱G1及G2。新制度從筆試合格日開始，在五年內要完成G牌，否則再由重考筆試開始。

LEVEL ONE DRIVER (G1)
第一階段（為期十二個月）

十六歲以上通過視力測驗及筆試。等候一年，學習駕駛，觀察馬路經驗才可以考路試。如曾修讀駕駛者訓練課程，等候期可減至八個月。

1. 除駕駛導師外，旁邊要有一位至少有四年開車經驗G牌的人陪同駕駛。

2. 除駕駛導師外，不准在主要的高速公路以及四百或四百多號的高速路上行駛及 Don Valley Parkway, Q.E.W. 等。

3. 午夜至凌晨五時不准駕駛。

4. 開車前不准喝酒駕駛，而陪同者的血液酒精含量不可高於 0.05 %。

5. 後座不准載超過安全帶數目的乘客，及最好有新駕駛者(New Driver)顯視牌。

6. 過了十二個月或八個月如通過路試合格後才能拿到第二階段的駕照即G2牌。

LEVEL TWO DRIVER (G2)
第二階段（為期十二個月）

1. 無須任何人陪同，可在任何時間及任何公路上駕駛。

2. 開車前不准喝酒。

3. 車上乘客數目必須配合安全帶的數量。

4. 在十二個月後再考G2路試，合格後才可獲全面駕駛執照G牌。

5. **青年人（即未滿20歲者）G2牌新法例**
   (在九月一日，二零零五年實施)

   G2牌青年駕駛者在深夜12時至晨早5時
   ▶ 在頭6個月只可乘載一位19歲或以下的乘客
   ▶ 在6個月後還未考獲G牌及還未滿20歲者，不准乘載超過 3 位 19 歲或以下的乘客

以上有些例外：
如坐在前排有一位四年或以上安省G牌人仕陪同或坐在車內的青年全是家庭成員。

注意：
1. 如果有證件及駕駛執照可證明本人有兩年或以上駕駛經驗者，當在考筆試前提交運輸處查閱，便不用等候，可立刻排期考G2或G1路試。

2. 如持有美國、日本、韓國、德國、法國、英國、奧地利、比利時、瑞士、加拿大其他省份或區域有效駕駛執照，兩年或以上者不需筆試及路試，可換安省牌照。

筆試過程及機器用法
How to use the Computerized Machine

1. 視力檢查

筆試者應能讀出驗眼機內的數目字及說出閃紅燈在左邊或右邊。

2. 考筆試

題目共四十題，其中交通符號及駕駛常識各佔二十題，每項不能錯多過四題，超過者必需重考（重考收費 $10）。

*用法 —— 細心看清楚試題，答案共有四個，例如 3 號是你選出的最佳答案，即按 3 字，肯定答案後，即按 OK，答案即會打出，如果是對的，下一條題目便出現，錯便會打出 "WRONG"。

3. 樣本題

1. 不平路在前面120公尺（400 呎）
2. 停牌在前面150公尺（500 呎）
3. 交通燈在前
4. 火車路在前

[1] [2] [3] [4] [OK]

1. BUMP 120 METERS (400 FEET) AHEAD
2. STOP SIGN 150 METERS (500 FEET) AHEAD
3. TRAFFIC SIGNS AHEAD
4. RAILWAY CROSSING AHEAD

ANSWER
答案
[3]

附圖是考英文或中文筆試用的電腦機

如以前有駕駛經驗者，請帶同你香港或原居地駕駛執照，可證明你己有多少月或兩年以上的經驗，可減少你日後路試等候期。

第一部份： 筆試 (Knowledge Test)

A) 交通符號 Traffic Signs
B) 駕駛常識 Knowledge for all Drivers

"Questions and Answers to pass the Knowledge Test"

考筆試共40條是非題：

A) 20題交通符號

B) 20題駕駛常識

(每項不能錯多過四題，超過者必須重考)

A) 交通符號　　Traffic Signs

1.

1. BUMP 120 METERS (400 FEET) AHEAD
2. STOP SIGN 150 METERS (500 FEET) AHEAD
3. TRAFFIC SIGNS AHEAD
4. RAILWAY CROSSING AHEAD

1. 不平路在前面120公尺（400呎）
2. 停牌在前面150公尺（500呎）
3. 交通燈在前
4. 火車路在前

3

2.

1. STOP SIGN AHEAD
2. YIELD RIGHT-OF-WAY
3. DEAD END STREET AHEAD
4. SLOW MOVING VEHICLE AHEAD

1. 停牌在前
2. 讓有優先權者先行
3. 前面是路的盡頭
4. 慢行的車輛在前

1

3.

1. DO NOT PASS ANY VEHICLES WITHIN 30 METERS OF A PEDESTRIAN CROSSING
2. SCHOOL ZONE
3. UNEVEN PAVEMENT AHEAD
4. CONSTRUCTION ZONE

1. 在斑馬線30公尺內不准超越其他車輛
2. 學校地區
3. 不平路面在前
4. 修路工程地帶

1

4.

1. NO RIGHT TURN
2. DIVIDED HIGHWAY ENDS
3. NARROW BRIDGE AHEAD
4. NO RIGHT TURN ON RED

1. 不可右轉
2. 分叉公路完或接合
3. 窄橋在前
4. 紅燈不可右轉

4

5.

1. YOU MUST MAKE A RIGHT TURN ONLY
2. YOU MUST NOT MAKE A LEFT TURN
3. HIDDEN INTERSECTION AHEAD
4. YOU ARE APPROACHING A TRAFFIC ISLAND

1. 你一定只可右轉
2. 你不准左轉
3. 隱蔽的十字路口在前
4. 你接近一個安全島

2

6.

1. YOU MAY EXIT IF YOU REMAIN IN RIGHT HAND LANE
2. YOU MUST NOT DRIVE IN RIGHT HAND LANE UNDER ANY CIRCUMSTANCES
3. END OF HIGHWAY, YOU MUST MOVE INTO RIGHT HAND LANE
4. TWO-WAY LEFT TURN LANE

1. 如果你保持在右線行駛，你可以駛出此公路
2. 在任何情形下，你不准在右線行駛
3. 公路終止，你一定要轉右線行駛
4. 兩邊轉左線

4

7.

1. INTERSECTION AHEAD
2. NARROW BRIDGE AHEAD
3. PAVED SURFACE ENDS AHEAD
4. THE ROAD AHEAD IS SPLIT

1. 十字路口在前
2. 窄橋在前
3. 前方道路完
4. 道路在前分叉

2

8.

1. PASS TO RIGHT OF TRAFFIC ISLAND
2. ROAD TURNS RIGHT THEN LEFT
3. WINDING ROAD AHEAD
4. PASS OTHER TRAFFIC ON THE RIGHT

1. 靠安全島的右面駛過
2. 路轉右然後轉左
3. 彎曲路在前
4. 在其他車輛右面駛過

1

9.

1. X-INTERSECTION FOR SCHOOL VEHICLES
2. SCHOOL CROSSWALK SIGN
3. CAUTION—SCHOOL BUS CROSSING
4. REGULATORY SIGN

1. 校車過的十字路口
2. 學校過斑馬線的標誌
3. 小心 — 學校巴士駛過
4. 限制路牌

4

10.

1. POLICEMEN AT INTERSECTION
2. YOU WILL GET A TICKET IF YOU DO NOT OBEY TRAFFIC SIGNAL
3. STOP FOR RED LIGHT AT INTERSECTION
4. RED LIGHT CAMERA AT INTERSECTION

1. 十字路口有警察看管
2. 你會有告票如不遵守交通燈號
3. 十字路口紅燈要停車
4. 十字路口安放紅燈照相機

4

11.

1. YOU ARE APPROACHING A FOUR-WAY INTERSECTION
2. YOU ARE APPROACHING A RAILROAD CROSSING
3. YOU ARE APPROACHING A HOSPITAL ZONE
4. YOU ARE APPROACHING A PEDESTRIAN CROSSWALK

1. 你接近一條十字路口
2. 你接近一條火車路
3. 你接近醫院地區
4. 你接近行人斑馬線

2

12.

1. TWO SEPARATE ROADS BY MEDIAN AHEAD, KEEP TO THE RIGHT
2. DIVIDED HIGHWAY ENDS
3. NARROW BRIDGE AHEAD
4. ROAD UNDER CONSTRUCTION

1. 前面有安全島分開兩面交通，靠右駛
2. 分叉公路完
3. 窄橋在前
4. 公路在修理中

1

3.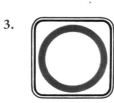

GREEN CIRCLE MEANS:
1. TRUCK ROUTE
2. NO TRUCKS
3. ROUTE FOR LARGE TRUCKS
4. PERMISSIVE SIGN

綠色圈的意思是：
1. 貨車路線
2. 不准貨車
3. 大貨車的路線
4. 准許的路牌

4

4.

1. A HIDDEN SCHOOL BUS STOP AHEAD, SLOW DOWN, DRIVE WITH EXTRA CAUTION, WATCH FOR CHILDREN AND SCHOOL BUSES WITH FLASHING RED LIGHTS
2. HIDDEN INTERSECTION
3. SCHOOL ZONE
4. SCHOOL WITH PLAY GROUND

1. 前面可能有隱藏的校巴，特別小心慢駛，留意小童及留意閃紅燈校巴
2. 隱藏十字路口
3. 學校區域
4. 學校及運動場

1

5.

1. STOP SIGN AHEAD
2. YIELD RIGHT-OF-WAY
3. DEAD END STREET AHEAD
4. SLOW MOVING VEHICLE

1. 停牌在前
2. 讓有優先權者先行
3. 前面是路的盡頭
4. 慢行的車輛

4

6.

1. SCHOOL AREA AHEAD
2. RAILWAY CROSSING AHEAD
3. YOU MUST GIVE THE RIGHT-OF-WAY
4. YOU HAVE THE RIGHT-OF-WAY

1. 學校區在前
2. 火車路在前
3. 你一定讓有優先權者先行
4. 你有優先權

3

7.

1. FACTORY, SLOW DOWN
2. BUMP OR UNEVEN PAVEMENT AHEAD
3. CONSTRUCTION ZONE
4. BRIDGE OR VIADUCT

1. 工廠在前，慢駛
2. 凹凸路或不平坦的路在前
3. 修路地區
4. 橋或橋樑

2

8.

1. ROAD SLIPPERY WHEN WET
2. NO RIGHT TURN PERMITTED
3. NO LEFT TURN PERMITTED
4. YOU MUST NOT MAKE A "U" TURN

1. 路濕時很滑
2. 不准右轉
3. 不准左轉
4. 你不准掉頭 (或 U 轉)

4

19.

1. LANE USAGE SIGN MEANING OF RIGHT TURN ONLY
2. LANE USAGE SIGN PERMITTING ALL TURNS INCLUDING LEFT
3. NO PARKING FROM ARROWS TO CORNER
4. ADVANCE WARNING OF DANGER

1. 此線只准右轉
2. 此線准許各方面轉彎包括左轉
3. 從箭的指示至角落，不准泊車
4. 特別警告危險

1

20.

1. DIVIDED HIGHWAY AHEAD
2. YOU ARE APPROACHING A ONE-WAY STREET
3. HIDDEN INTERSECTION AHEAD
4. PAVEMENT NARROWS

1. 分叉公路在前
2. 你正接近一條單程路
3. 隱蔽路口在前
4. 路面轉窄

4

21.

1. TRUCK ENTRANCE ON THE RIGHT SIDE AHEAD
2. NO TRUCKS ALLOWED
3. SLOW DOWN FOR TRUCK
4. TRUCK ROUTE

1. 前右邊有貨車出入口
2. 貨車不可進入
3. 見到貨車時要減速
4. 貨車專線

1

22.

1. DESTINATION BOARD
2. SCHOOL ZONE—WATCH FOR CHILDREN PLAYING
3. PROVINCIAL PARK
4. PEDESTRIAN CONTROL SIGN

1. 目的地指示牌
2. 學校區 — 小心兒童玩耍
3. 省公園
4. 行人路牌

1

23.

RED CIRCLE MEANS:
1. DO NOT ENTER ROADWAY
2. DO NOT ENTER UNLESS LOCAL TRAFFIC
3. A TRAFFIC CIRCLE AHEAD
4. PROHIBITED SIGN

紅色圈的意思是：
1. 不准駛入此路
2. 不准駛入除非區內居民
3. 前面有一交通圈
4. 禁止路牌

4

24.

1. DRIVE WITH CAUTION
2. SHARE THE ROAD WITH ONCOMING TRAFFIC
3. SLIPPERY WHEN WET
4. NO STANDING

1. 小心駕駛
2. 與對路車分享道路
3. 路面濕時很滑
4. 不可停車

2

5.

1. NARROW ROAD AHEAD
2. ROAD AHEAD TURNS LEFT THEN RIGHT
3. ROAD AHEAD TURNS RIGHT THEN LEFT
4. INTERSECTION AHEAD

1. 窄路在前
2. 前面的路轉左然後轉右
3. 前面的路轉右然後轉左
4. 十字路口在前

`3`

6.

1. NO ENTRY INTO INTERSECTION
2. THIS SIGN MEANS NO STOPPING
3. VEHICLES APPROACHING FROM THE ANGLE SHOWN, MUST STOP
4. NEED NOT STOP FOR STOP SIGNS IN DIRECTION OF ARROWS

1. 十字路口，不准駛入
2. 不准停車牌
3. 汽車駛向此箭咀，一定要停
4. 停牌所指示的方向不需要停

`2`

7.

1. MAXIMUM SPEED OF 50 KM (30 MILES) PER HOUR FROM THIS SIGN TO NEXT SIGN
2. SPEED LIMIT FOR RURAL SCHOOL ZONES
3. END OF 50 KM (30 MILES) PER HOUR ZONE
4. MAXIMUM SPEED OF 50 KM (30 MILES) PER HOUR AHEAD

1. 由此牌至下一路牌，最高時速每小時五十公里（三十哩）
2. 鄉村學校區內的時速
3. 每小時五十公里（三十哩）完
4. 前面時速每小時可達五十公里（三十哩）

`4`

28.

1. CONSTRUCTION SIGN—SLOW DOWN OBEY FLAGMAN'S DIRECTION
2. A CONSTRUCTION SIGN REPLACING FLAGMAN ON DUTY
3. REGULATORY SIGN—REDUCE SPEED
4. THIS SIGN WARNS OF ROAD WORK OPERATION AHEAD

1. 修路的標誌 — 慢駛服從修路者旗的指示
2. 以修路標誌代替修路者旗的指示
3. 限制路牌 — 減低速度
4. 此牌警告公路修理工程在前

`4`

29.

1. DO NOT COME NEAR
2. NEW BORN BABY ON BOARD
3. NEW DRIVER
4. NEW CAR

1. 不可接近
2. 新嬰兒在車上
3. 新駕駛者
4. 新車

`3`

30.

1. HIDDEN INTERSECTION AHEAD
2. WINDING ROAD
3. ROAD SLIPPERY WHEN WET
4. NARROW ROAD AHEAD

1. 隱蔽的十字路口在前
2. 彎曲路
3. 路濕時很滑
4. 窄路在前

`2`

31.

1. THIS LANE IS RESERVED FOR SPECIFIC TYPES OF VEHICLES DURING CERTAIN TIMES AND DAYS SUCH AS BUSES, TAXIS, BICYCLES AND VEHICLES WITH MORE THAN THREE PASSENGERS
2. NO BUSES ALLOWED ON SPECIFIED LANE DURING POSTED TIMES AND DAYS
3. NO STOPPING WITHIN THE TIMES AND DAYS
4. DO NOT ENTER BETWEEN THE TIMES AND DAYS

1. 這線是保留於專線車輛，如巴士、的士、腳踏車及車上有三名乘客以上在指定時間、日期專用
2. 在指定時間及日期，巴士是不准在專線行駛
3. 在指定時間及日期，是不准停車的
4. 在指定時間及日期，是不准駛入的

1

32.

1. KEEP TO RIGHT
2. KEEP TO LEFT
3. KEEP OUT (DO NOT ENTER)
4. DO NOT PASS

1. 靠右行駛
2. 靠左行駛
3. 不准駛入
4. 不准超越

3

33.

1. WINDING ROAD AHEAD
2. BUMPY ROAD AHEAD
3. ROAD AHEAD SLIPPERY WHEN WET
4. NO PASSING AHEAD

1. 彎曲路在前
2. 不平路在前
3. 前路濕時很滑
4. 前面不准超越

3

34.

1. CARE FOR PEDESTRIAN
2. WATCH FOR TRAFFIC SIGNAL
3. DO NOT BLOCK INTERSECTION
4. DO NOT SLOW DOWN

1. 小心行人
2. 十字路口注意交通燈號
3. 不可在十字路口上阻塞交通
4. 不可在十字路口減慢速度

3

35.

1. YOU MAY EXIT IF YOU REMAIN IN RIGHT HAND LANE
2. YOU MUST NOT DRIVE IN RIGHT HAND LANE UNDER ANY CIRCUMSTANCES
3. END OF HIGHWAY, YOU MUST MOVE INTO RIGHT HAND LANE
4. YOU MUST EXIT IF YOU REMAIN IN RIGHT HAND LANE

1. 如果你保持在右線行駛，你可以駛出此公路
2. 在任何情形下，你不准在右線行駛
3. 公路終止，你一定要轉右線行駛
4. 如果你保持在右線行駛，你一定要駛出此路

4

6.

1. STOP SIGN 150 METERS (500 FEET) AHEAD
2. BUMP 120 METERS (400 FEET) AHEAD
3. STOP AT ALL TIMES
4. STOP ONLY IF OTHER VEHICLES ARE APPROACHING

1. 停牌在前面150 公尺（500呎）
2. 不平路在前面120 公尺（400呎）
3. 任何時間都必要停車
4. 當接近別的車輛時才停

3

7.

1. BY WHEEL-CHAIR ONLY OR DISABLED PERSON PARKING (HANDICAP)
2. WINDING ROAD AHEAD
3. NO PARKING
4. NO STANDING

1. 輪椅或傷殘人停泊
2. 彎曲路在前
3. 不准停泊
4. 不准站留

1

8.

1. I AM TURNING RIGHT
2. I AM TURNING LEFT
3. I AM SLOWING OR STOPPING
4. YOU MAY PASS ME

1. 我正在右轉
2. 我正在左轉
3. 我正在慢下或停車
4. 你可以超越我

1

9.

1. DEER REGULARLY CROSS, BE ALERT FOR ANIMALS
2. ZOO AHEAD
3. NO HONKING AT ANIMALS
4. DEER ARE WELCOME

1. 警覺動物，鹿有時橫過
2. 動物園在前
3. 見到動物不准按喇叭
4. 鹿群歡迎的

1

40.

1. WINDING ROAD AHEAD
2. KEEP TO LEFT
3. DANGER, ROAD ENDS
4. DANGER, SHARP TURN

1. 彎曲路在前
2. 靠左
3. 危險，路的盡頭
4. 危險，急彎

4

41.

1. DIVIDED HIGHWAY AHEAD
2. DIVIDED HIGHWAY ENDS
3. NARROW BRIDGE AHEAD
4. ROAD UNDER CONSTRUCTION

1. 分叉公路在前
2. 分叉公路完
3. 窄橋在前
4. 公路在修理中

2

42.

1. I AM TURNING LEFT
2. I AM SLOWING OR STOPPING
3. I AM TURNING RIGHT
4. YOU MAY PASS ME

1. 我正在轉左
2. 我正在慢駛或停車
3. 我正在轉右
4. 你可以超越我

2

43.

1. NARROW ROAD AHEAD
2. HIDDEN INTERSECTION AHEAD
3. RAILWAY CROSSING AHEAD
4. INTERSECTION AHEAD, THE ARROW SHOWS WHICH DIRECTION OF TRAFFIC HAS THE RIGHT-OF-WAY

1. 窄路在前
2. 隱藏路在前
3. 火車路在前
4. 十字路口在前，箭頭路有優先權

4

44.

1. SAFETY CHECK AHEAD
2. WARNS OF A STEEP HILL AHEAD
3. PAVEMENT ENDS, 500 FEET AHEAD
4. BUMPY ROAD AHEAD

1. 前面有安全檢查
2. 警告斜坡在前
3. 路在前面五百呎終止
4. 不平路在前

2

45.

1. SCHOOL AREA
2. BUMPY ROAD
3. DO NOT STAND OR STOP IN THIS AREA
4. NO BICYCLE ALLOWED ON THIS ROAD

1. 學校區
2. 不平坦的路
3. 不准站或停在這處
4. 腳踏車不准行駛

3

46.

1. RIGHT LANE ENDS
2. HIDDEN INTERSECTION AHEAD
3. YOU ARE APPROACHING STEEP HILL
4. PEDESTRIAN CROSSING AHEAD

1. 右線終止
2. 隱蔽的十字路口在前
3. 你正接近一斜坡
4. 行人斑馬線在前

1

47.

1. I AM TURNING RIGHT
2. I AM TURNING LEFT
3. I AM SLOWING OR STOPPING
4. I AM STOPPING

1. 我正在轉右
2. 我正在轉左
3. 我正在慢駛或停車
4. 我正在停車

2

8.

1. RIGHT LANE ENDS
2. HIDDEN INTERSECTION AHEAD
3. YOU ARE APPROACHING STEEP HILL
4. PASSING IS NOT ALLOWED

1. 右線終止
2. 隱蔽的十字路口在前
3. 你正接近一斜坡
4. 不准超越

4

9.

1. PLAYGROUND ZONE SIGN
2. CHILDREN PLAYING IN RESIDENTIAL AREA
3. SCHOOL ZONE SIGN
4. DIRECTION SIGN FOR CHILDREN

1. 遊樂場的路牌
2. 兒童在住宅區玩耍
3. 學校區的路牌
4. 指示兒童的路牌

3

0.

1. NO SMOKING
2. NOT MORE THAN 3 MINUTES IDLING
3. IDLING IS PERMITTED
4. NO STOPPING MORE THAN 3 MINUTES

1. 不准吸煙
2. 不准停下開動汽車超過三分鐘
3. 停下開動汽車是許可的
4. 不准停在這裡超過三分鐘

2

1.

1. WHEN A SCHOOL BUS ARM SWINGS OUT WITH RED LIGHTS FLASHING, YOU MUST STOP AND YOU ARE PROHIBITED FROM PASSING
2. CONSTRUCTION SIGN
3. SCHOOL ZONE
4. STOP SIGN AHEAD

1. 當學校巴士停牌伸出時亦閃著紅燈，你應停下及不准超越
2. 修路工程地帶
3. 學校區域
4. 前面有停牌

1

52.

1. IT IS A WARNING SIGN
2. DURING SCHOOL HOURS WHEN THE YELLOW LIGHTS ARE FLASHING, FOLLOW THE SPEED LIMIT SHOWN
3. WATCH FOR CROSS GUARD ONLY
4. WATCH FOR CHILDREN ONLY

1. 這是一個警告牌
2. 在學生上課時間內，當閃著黃燈時，汽車要跟路牌速度行駛
3. 只小心幫助學童過馬路的護衛者
4. 只小心兒童

2

53.

1. HIGHWAY WITH TWO EXPRESS LANES
2. THE TWO LANES AHEAD ARE CLOSED
3. TWO OR MORE PASSENGERS MUST BE IN THE VEHICLE TO USE THIS LANE ON THE HIGHWAY (HOV SIGN)
4. TWO LANES WILL MERGE INTO ONE

1. 高速公路上有兩條特快線
2. 前面兩條線快完
3. 在公路上使用這線必須車上有兩人或以上者
4. 兩條線會合成一條

3

1. **When does the law require lights on vehicles to be turned on?**

1. Between sunset and sunrise
2. Between dusk and dawn and at any other time you cannot see clearly for a distance of 150 m (500 ft.)
3. Between half an hour before sunset to half an hour after sunrise and at any other time you cannot see clearly for a distance of 150 m (500 ft.)
4. No specified time

1. **法律上，在什麼時候需要把車頭燈開著？**

1. 在日落和日出時
2. 在黃昏及黎明之間和在任何時間150公尺（500呎）內看不清楚時
3. 在日落前半小時，在日出後半小時及任何時間在150公尺（500呎）內看不清楚事物時
4. 沒有特別時間規定

3

2. **In what position on the roadway must you be before making a left turn from a one-way traffic street?**

1. Close to the right-hand side of the roadway
2. Close to the centre line of the roadway
3. Close to the left side of the roadway
4. Does not matter provided you signal

2. **在單程路上你想轉左之前，你應在路的什麼位置？**

1. 靠近路的右手邊
2. 靠近路的中線
3. 靠近路的左手邊
4. 不成問題，只要你打訊號

3

3. **When two cars reach an uncontrolled intersection at approximately the same time, the right-of-way should be given to:**

1. The one approaching from the left
2. The one approaching from the right
3. Neither one
4. The one moving faster

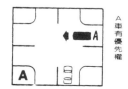

3. **當兩架車在大約同一時間駛到沒有標誌的十字路口，那一架車有優先權？**

1. 從左方駛來的車輛
2. 從右方駛來的車輛
3. 兩者都不是
4. 駛得較快的車輛

2

4. When a streetcar stops to take on or discharge passengers, where there is no safety zone, what does the law require you to do before passing the streetcar?

1. Stop behind the rear of the streetcar and then proceed
2. Sound horn and pass with caution
3. Pass on the left side when the way is clear
4. Stop 2 m (6 ft.) behind the rearmost door where passengers are getting on or off, and proceed only when it is safe to do so

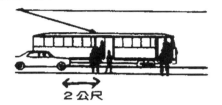

4. 當電車停下讓乘客上落，當時沒有安全島，你想駛過電車前，法律上要你怎樣做？

1. 停在電車後面，然後前進
2. 響號，同時小心駛過
3. 由左邊駛過，當交通安全
4. 在電車後門2公尺(6呎)之後停車，讓乘客上落，直至安全才駛過

4

5. When it is safe to do so, passing other vehicles on the right side:

1. Is permitted on any street or highway
2. Is permitted providing it is possible to do so by driving on the shoulder of the road
3. Is not permitted under any circumstances
4. Is permitted when the street or highway has two or more lanes for traffic in the direction you are travelling

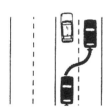

5. 在安全的情形下，可從別的車輛右方超越：

1. 任何街道及公路都准許
2. 如果可能在路旁駛過是准許的
3. 無論在什麼情況下都不准許
4. 是准許的，當街道及公路有兩條或以上同一方向的行車線

4

6. Which of the following has the right-of-way over all others at an intersection when the signal light is green?

1. Pedestrians crossing against the light
2. Pedestrians crossing with the light
3. Vehicles turning right
4. Vehicles turning left

6. 在十字路口亮綠燈時，以下誰最有優先權？

1. 行人不守燈號過馬路
2. 行人遵守燈號過馬路
3. 正在轉右的車輛
4. 正在轉左的車輛

2

7. **On a roadway where traffic is moving in both directions, in what position must you be before making a left turn?**
   1. Close to the right-hand side of the roadway
   2. Close to the left side of the roadway
   3. Immediately to the right of the centre line of the roadway
   4. Does not matter provided you signal

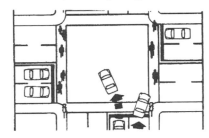

7. **在雙程路上，你想轉左之前，你應在什麼位置？**
   1. 靠近路的右手邊
   2. 靠近路的左手邊
   3. 盡量在最接近中線的右邊行車路上
   4. 沒有關係，只要打燈號便可

   3

8. **When a red signal light with a green arrow is shown at an intersection it means:**
   1. Stop and wait for the green light before making a turn in the direction of the arrow
   2. Proceed with caution in the direction of the arrow, yielding right-of-way to pedestrians and other traffic
   3. Stop and then proceed
   4. The green arrow is a signal for pedestrians only

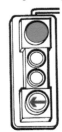

8. **在十字路口，亮紅燈並有綠色箭咀表示：**
   1. 停，先等候綠燈，然後向綠色箭咀的方向轉
   2. 小心向著箭咀的方向轉，讓路與有優先權的車輛及行人
   3. 停車，然後前進
   4. 綠色箭咀只是給行人的訊號

   2

9. **When entering a freeway you should:**
   1. Stop on acceleration lane, wait for an opening, then enter the freeway rapidly
   2. Accelerate quickly to freeway speed and merge with freeway traffic
   3. Slow down, and then enter freeway at a sharp angle
   4. Drive slowly and be prepared to stop for freeway traffic

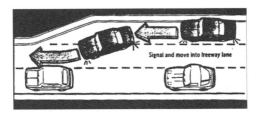

Signal and move into freeway lane

9. **當駛入高速公路時，你應該：**
   1. 停在加速線，看準有安全的位置才盡快駛入高速公路
   2. 加速達到高速公路的速度，然後駛入公路交通中
   3. 慢車，然後用直角方向駛入高速公路
   4. 慢駛，隨時準備停下來應付公路的交通

   2

10. Every accident must be reported to the police where there is personal injury or when the damage exceeds:
   1. $100
   2. $150
   3. $1500
   4. $1000

10. 一定要報警的交通意外是當有人受傷或損失超過：
   1. 一百元
   2. 一百五十元
   3. 一千五百元
   4. 一千元

4

11. While travelling on a highway, the driver of a motor vehicle is not permitted to carry _____ in a house or boat trailer:
   1. Firearms
   2. Flammable material
   3. Persons (Passenger)
   4. Pets

11. 在公路，駕駛者不准在其汽車所拖的露營車或拖船上載有：
   1. 鎗械
   2. 容易燃燒原料
   3 人（乘客）
   4. 家畜

3

12. At what level of alcohol in the blood can you be convicted of being an impaired driver?
   1. 0.03%
   2. 0.05%
   3. 0.08%
   4. 1.0%

12. 酒精在人體血液中佔什麼份量，使你成為危險駕駛者及有罪?
   1. 0.03%
   2. 0.05%
   3. 0.08%
   4. 1.0%

IF YOU DRINK, DON'T DRIVE.

3

13. In Ontario, there is a seat belt law?

1. Yes
2. No
3. Only when driving on an open highway
4. Only when driving within a municipality

13. 在安大略省，是有安全帶法例？

1. 對
2. 不對
3. 只是在公路上駕駛時
4. 只是在市區內駕駛時

`1`

14. When lights are required, drivers must use lower beam headlights when following another vehicle:

1. Within 30 m (100 ft.)
2. Within 60 m (200 ft.)
3. Within 120 m (400 ft.)
4. This only applies when approaching another vehicle

14. 當需要開車頭燈時，駕駛者必要用低燈，當跟在別的車後面：

1. 30公尺（100呎）內
2. 60公尺（200呎）內
3. 120公尺（400呎）內
4. 只是當接近其他車輛時

`2`

15. If the signal light changes from green to amber as you approach an intersection, what should you do?

1. Stop. If stop cannot be made safely proceed with caution
2. Speed up to clear the intersection as quickly as possible
3. Continue through intersection without slowing or stopping
4. Sound horn to warm pedestrians and other drivers that you do not intend to stop

15. 當到達十字路口，綠燈剛轉黃燈，你應怎樣做？

1. 停車，如果停車是危險的，前進，但要加倍小心
2. 加速，並盡快駛過十字路口
3. 繼續駛過十字路口，不用慢駛或停下來
4. 響號，並警告行人和別的駕駛者，使他們知道你不會停車

`1`

16. Upon approaching a Yield-sign, what does the law require you to do?

1. Slow down, stop if necessary, and yield right-of-way
2. Stop, then enter traffic slowly
3. Stop, then enter traffic quickly
4. Speed up and force your way into traffic

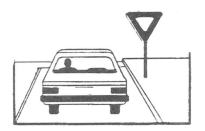

16. 當駛近 "讓牌" 時，在法例上你應怎樣做？

1. 慢下，如有需要時停下及讓路與有優先權者先行
2. 停，然後慢駛入交通中
3. 停，然後快速駛入交通中
4. 加速，並擠迫入交通中

1

17. A person whose driver's licence is under suspension, may:

1. Operate a motor vehicle in a case of extreme emergency
2. Operate a motor vehicle to and from work
3. Operate a motor vehicle when accompanied by a licensed driver
4. Not operate a motor vehicle under any conditions

17. 某人的駕駛執照被吊銷後，他……

1. 在非常緊急時，可以駕駛
2. 返工及放工時才准駕駛
3. 在有車牌的人陪同下才可駕駛
4. 在任何情形下都不准駕駛

4

18. Are drivers responsible for their passengers buckling up?

1. Only if passengers are over sixteen years of age
2. Only if passengers are from five years of age up to sixteen
3. Only if the passengers are in the front seat
4. Only if passengers are over eighteen years of age

18. 駕駛者是否要負責車上乘客扣上安全帶呢？

1. 只是乘客在十六歲以上
2. 只是乘客在五歲至十六歲
3. 只是乘客在前面的座位
4. 只是乘客在十八歲以上

2

19. **Before leaving your car parked on a downgrade, you should:**
   1. Leave your front wheels parallel to the curb
   2. Turn your front wheels to the left and set your parking brake
   3. Set your parking brake only
   4. Turn your front wheels to the right and set your parking brake

19. **當你泊車在向下的斜坡時，在你離開車之前，你應：**
   1. 扭直前胎與路邊平行
   2. 扭前胎向左，並拉緊手掣
   3. 只要拉緊手掣
   4. 扭前胎向右，並拉緊手掣

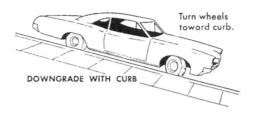

Turn wheels toward curb.

DOWNGRADE WITH CURB

4

20. **When a right turn against a red signal light is permitted, what does the law require you to do before entering the intersection and making the turn?**
   1. Slow down, proceed with caution
   2. Stop, then edge into traffic
   3. Stop, signal, make the turn so as not to interfere with other traffic, including pedestrians
   4. Slow down, signal and turn

20. **當紅燈可以轉右時，在未駛入十字路口前，法律上你應怎樣做？**
   1. 慢駛，小心前進
   2. 停車，然後側側地進入交通中
   3. 停車，打燈號、當不阻礙別的車輛及行人才轉彎
   4. 慢駛，打訊號及轉彎

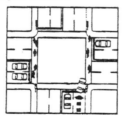

3

21. **The best way to stop quickly on a wet or icy roadway is to:**
   1. Pump the brake until you come to a stop
   2. Keep foot off brake and let compression stop you
   3. Step on brakes hard and try to prevent vehicle from skidding
   4. Apply brakes the same way you always do

21. **在濕滑或結冰的路上快速停車的最好方法是：**
   1. 在腳掣上一踏一放的方法，直至車輛完全停下來
   2. 把腳離開腳掣，使車自動停下
   3. 大力踏在腳掣上，預防車輛滑行
   4. 像你平時一樣方法踏腳掣

1

22. In what lane of traffic should you drive when you intend to make a right-hand turn?

1. Close to the left side of the roadway
2. Close to the right-hand side of the roadway
3. Close to the centre line of the roadway
4. Does not matter provided you signal

22. 當你想轉右時，你應駛在路的那一條線？

1. 靠近路的左邊
2. 靠近路的右邊
3. 靠近路的中線
4. 不成問題，打燈便可

2

23. When driving in heavy fog, you should use:

1. Parking lights
2. Low beam headlights
3. Parking lights and high beam headlights
4. High beam headlights

23. 在大霧中行駛，你應用：

1. 泊車燈
2. 低燈
3. 泊車燈及高燈
4. 高燈

2

24. A flashing red signal light at an intersection means:

1. Slow down and drive with increased caution
2. Slow down and if necessary yield right-of-way to cars approaching from the left or right
3. Signal light is out of order, proceed with caution
4. Stop. Proceed only when it is safe to do so

24. 在十字路口閃著紅燈，表示：

1. 慢駛，然後加倍小心駕駛
2. 慢駛，如有需要，讓左右迎面的車輛有優先權
3. 燈號壞了，小心前進
4. 停車，直至安全才前進

4

25. As a level one or level two driver, if you collect nine or more points during a two-year period, your licence will be suspended for?
 1. 60 days
 2. 30 days
 3. 1 year
 4. 15 days

25. 在兩年間第一階段及第二階段駕駛者，如你的過失點在九分或以上，你會停牌多久?
 1. 60天
 2. 30天
 3. 一年
 4. 15天

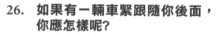

9 Points

1

26. If someone is tailgating you what should you do?
 1. Move into another lane when it is safe to do so
 2. Slow down slightly to increase the space in front of your car
 3. Pull over to let the tailgater pass
 4. All of the above

26. 如果有一輛車緊跟隨你後面，你應怎樣呢?
 1. 如果安全時，轉去其他行車線
 2. 輕微地減慢與前面的車輛增遠距離
 3. 駛近路旁讓緊跟隨車超越
 4. 以上全部都是

 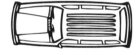

27. To get your vehicle out of a skid, you should first: (e.g. your rear wheels suddenly slip to the right)
 1. Steer in the opposite direction of the skid
 2. Steer straight ahead
 3. Apply brake hard
 4. Steer in the direction of the skid

27. 當你的汽車滑胎時，首先怎樣應付：（例如車尾滑向右邊）
 1. 把方向盤轉向相反滑車的方向
 2. 把方向盤轉直走
 3. 大力煞停汽車
 4. 把方向盤轉向滑車的方向

4

28. If you want to pass a motorcycle, you should:

1. Honk your horn before you pass
2. Turn on your high-beam lights before you pass
3. Pass just as you would with another car
4. Use half of their lane to pass

28. 如果你想超越一部摩托車，你應：

1. 在超越前響號
2. 在超越前將你的高燈開亮
3. 方法像超越其他車輛
4. 用摩托車的一半行車線

29. If you lose control of your vehicle and it goes off the road, you should:

1. Grip the steering wheel firmly
2. Take your foot off the gas pedal to slow down and avoid heavy breaking
3. When the vehicle is under control steer back to the road
4. All of the above

29. 在駕駛時，如果你失控，車胎駛出路邊，你應：

1. 緊握方向盤
2. 腳離開油門使車速放慢，避免重踏腳掣
3. 當車得到控掣後駛回車路上
4. 以上全部都是

4

30. Under the Criminal Code, if you are caught driving while your licence is suspended, your vehicle will be impounded for?

1. 1 year
2. 6 months
3. 45 days
4. 30 days

30. 如果你是"犯刑事法"停牌，而被捉駕駛，你的汽車會扣押多久？

1. 一年
2. 6個月
3. 45天
4. 30天

3

31. The police have the right to stop any driver they suspect is impaired. If you refuse to take a breathalyzer test, your licence will be suspended immediately for:
1. 30 days
2. 1 year
3. 60 days
4. 90 days

31. 警察有權截查可疑醉酒駕駛者，如你拒絕用酒精測試器，你的車牌會立刻吊銷到：
1. 30天
2. 1年
3. 60天
4. 90天

90 Days

4

32. When on streets designed for two-way traffic, you hear the siren of an emergency vehicle, what does the law require you to do?
1. Speed up and get out of the way
2. Signal the driver to pass
3. Pull to the right as far as possible and stop
4. Continue at same speed

32. 當你在雙線行車路上駕駛，聽到緊急響號的車，法律上要求你怎樣做？
1. 加速，盡快離開
2. 打燈號，讓駕駛者超越
3. 盡快駛向路的最右方停下
4. 保持同一速度行駛

AMBULANCE

3

33. Snow tires are good for:
1. Summer driving
2. All season driving
3. Winter driving
4. Spring and fall only

33. 雪胎甚麼時候用最好：
1. 在夏天駕駛
2. 在四季都可
3. 在冬天駕駛
4. 在春天及秋天用

雪胎

3

34. When lights are required, drivers are required to use low beam headlights?
1. Within 1 km (0.6 mile) of the approach of another vehicle
2. Within 150 m (500 ft.) of the approach of another vehicle
3. Within 300 m (1000 ft.) of the approach of another vehicle
4. This is a safety practice, not a law

34. 當需要車頭燈時，在什麼情形下需要開低燈?
1. 與最接近你的車輛相距一公里(0.6哩)內
2. 與最接近你的車輛相距150公尺(500呎)內
3. 與最接近你的車輛相距300公尺(1000呎)內
4. 這是為安全而設，並不是法律規定

2

35. Under the Highway Traffic Act, if you are convicted of driving while your licence is suspended, assuming it is your first offence, you will:
1. Receive a fine of $500
2. Be fined between $1000 to $5000
3. Be sentenced to six months in jail
4. All of the above

35. 在公路交通法規被停牌，而你是第一次被捉駕駛，刑罰是:
1. 罰款500元
2. 罰款1000元至5000元
3. 坐監6個月
4. 以上全部都是

2

36. At an intersection where there is a flashing amber (yellow) traffic light, you must:
1. Stop if making right turn
2. Continue at same speed
3. Stop if making left turn
4. Slow down and proceed with caution

閃黃燈   A Flashing amber (yellow)

36. 當你到達十字路口而看到黃色的閃燈時，你一定要:
1. 停車，如果你想轉右
2. 保持同樣的速度行駛
3. 停車，如果你想轉左
4. 慢駛，然後小心前進

4

37. Never change lanes in traffic without:

1. Giving proper signal and looking to make sure the move can be made safely
2. Decreasing speed and giving correct signal
3. Looking into the rear view mirror only
4. Blowing your horn and looking to the rear

37. 不能隨時換線除非事先：

1. 發出正確燈號及肯定安全才能轉線
2. 減慢速度及打出正確燈號
3. 只看倒後鏡
4. 響喇叭及望後面

38. Under what circumstances may a driver's licence be cancelled?

1. For failure to attend for re-examination
2. For possession of an altered driver's licence
3. For failure to satisfactorily complete a driver re-examination
4. Any or all of the above

38. 在什麼情形下，駕駛執照會被取消？

1. 沒有去重考
2. 持有改過的執照
3. 重考而不合格
4. 以上任何情形或全部都是

39. When selling a motor vehicle to another person, you, the seller, should:

1. Notify the Ministry of the change of ownership within six days of date of sale
2. Go with the buyer to a vehicle licence issuing office to carry out the change of ownership
3. If selling the vehicle without a Safety Standards Certificate, you must return the vehicle licence plates and motor vehicle permit to a vehicle licence issuing office and obtain an Unfit Vehicle Permit in the buyer's name
4. All of the above

39. 賣汽車給別人，賣車者應該：

1. 在賣車後六日內通知交通部及改車主姓名
2. 和買車者到換牌處登記更換新車主姓名
3. 如汽車沒有「安全合格證」應交還車牌及車證給換牌處，而用買車者的名下取得「汽車未合格證」
4. 以上所有情形都是

40. What documents may a police officer require a motor vehicle owner to produce?

1. If the motor vehicle is insured—a liability insurance card
2. The motor vehicle ownership
3. If he/she is operating a motor vehicle—a valid driver's licence
4. Any of the above

40. 警察有權要求車主拿出什麼文件?

ANSWER 答案

1. 如汽車有買保險 — 保險紙
2. 汽車車主證
3. 如他/她是汽車駕駛者 — 有效駕駛執照
4. 以上任何一項都是

4

41. You should, under all condition, drive at a speed which will allow you to:

1. Stop within 90 meters (300 feet)
2. Stop within 60 meters (200 feet)
3. Stop within a safe distance
4. Stop within 150 meters (500 feet)

41. 你應保持一種均衡速度行車,無論在任何情況下,你也能:

1. 在90公尺(300呎)內停車
2. 在60公尺(200呎)內停車
3. 在一個安全距離內停車
4. 在150公尺(500呎)內停車

3

42. What insurance protection does the owner get who pays the uninsured motor vehicle fee?

1. $10,000 insurance coverage
2. $20,000 insurance coverage
3. $35,000 insurance coverage
4. No insurance protection whatever

42. 如果車主沒有買汽車保險,他有什麼保障?

1. 一萬元保險賠償
2. 二萬元保險賠償
3. 三萬五千元保險賠償
4. 全無保險保障

4

43. Which of the following penalties can the court impose on a person convicted of driving 50 km/h (30 m.p.h.) or more over the speed limit?

1. Suspension of licence for 6 months
2. Suspension of licence for 30 days and/or fine up to $10,000
3. Impoundment of motor vehicle for 6 months
4. Imprisonment of person for 6 months

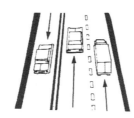

43. 駕駛者犯上開快車，比限制時速超過五十公里（三十哩）或以上時，法庭將會怎樣處罰呢？

1. 停牌六個月
2. 停牌三十天及/或罰款在一萬元以下
3. 扣留汽車六個月
4. 駕駛者入獄六個月

2

44. As a level one (G1) driver, you must be accompanied by a class G or higher licenced driver, who has the following driving experience more than:

1. Three years
2. Four years
3. Eight years
4. Six years

44. 第一階段駕駛者，你一定要有一個G牌或以上陪同駕駛，他的駕駛經驗在幾多年以上：

1. 3年
2. 4年
3. 8年
4. 6年

4 Years

2

45. When may you lend your driver's licence?

1. Never
2. To another person who is learning to drive
3. For identification purposes only
4. In emergencies

45. 在什麼情形下可將駕駛執照借給他人？

1. 永遠不可
2. 可以借給正在學車者
3. 只可作表明身份用
4. 在緊急時

1

46. Overdriving your headlights at night is dangerous because:

1. You are driving too fast
2. Your headlights are too bright
3. You cannot stop within the distance that you can see
4. It is not good for the car battery

46. 在晚間駕駛，如車速快過你的車頭燈所照到的是危險，因為：

1. 你駛車太快
2. 你的車頭燈太亮
3. 你看到時，想停也停不下來
4. 這是對汽車電池不好的

3

47. When approaching an intersection where a traffic signal light is red and a policeman motions you to go through, you should:

1. Wait for the light to turn green
2. Obey the policeman's signal and go through at once
3. Call the policeman's attention to the red light
4. Stop to make sure he/she wants you to go through

47. 當你駛近十字路口，正亮紅色交通燈，而警察打手勢指揮你通過，你應：

1. 等候綠燈
2. 服從警察的指揮，立即通過
3. 讓警察知道當時亮紅燈
4. 停下來，確定他要你通過

2

48. When a car stops to allow a pedestrian to cross the street at a marked crosswalk, you should:

1. Pass the stopped car on the left
2. Sound horn for the driver of the stopped car to drive on
3. Pass the stopped car to the right
4. Not pass any car stopped to allow a pedestrian to cross

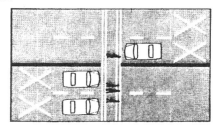

48. 當車輛停下來讓行人過斑馬線時，你應：

1. 從左面超越停下的車
2. 響號指使停車的駕駛者向前駛
3. 從右面超越停下的車
4. 不准超越任何車輛，停下來讓行人過馬路

4

49. When a truck becomes disabled on the highway, where the speed limit is in excess of 60 km/h, flares or reflectors must be placed approximately what distance ahead of and to the rear of this disabled vehicle?

1. 15 m (50 ft.)
2. 30 m (100 ft.)
3. 60 m (200 ft.)
4. 90 m (300 ft.)

49. 當貨車在高速公路上不能開動時，照明器或反光器一定要放在貨車的前面或後面多遠呢？

1. 15公尺（50呎）
2. 30公尺（100呎）
3. 40公尺（200呎）
4. 90公尺（300呎）

2

50. Unless otherwise posted, the maximum speed limit allowed in cities, town, villages and built-up area is:

1. 30 km/h (20 m.p.h.)
2. 50 km/h (30 m.p.h.)
3. 40 km/h (25 m.p.h.)
4. 60 km/h (35 m.p.h.)

MAXIMUM
50
km/h

50. 除非有標誌指明，不然在城市、市鎮、鄉村或發展區內最高的駕駛速度是：

1. 每小時30公里（20哩）
2. 每小時50公里（30哩）
3. 每小時40公里（25哩）
4. 每小時60公里（35哩）

2

51. How soon, after a licensed driver changes his/her name or address, is he/she required to notify the Ministry of Transportation and Communications?

1. Within 6 days
2. Within 15 days
3. Within 30 days
4. At any time prior to renewal of licence

6 Days

51. 持有駕駛執照而需要轉姓名或地址，他需要在什麼時間內通知交通部？

1. 六天內
2. 十五天內
3. 三十天內
4. 在換新牌前任何時間都可

1

52. When the traffic signal light facing you is red and you intend to go straight through the intersection, what must you do?

1. Stop, give pedestrians the right-of-way, then proceed with caution
2. Stop, proceed when the way is clear
3. Slow down, proceed when the way is clear
4. Stop, proceed only when the signal turns green and when the way is clear

52. 當亮紅燈時，你想駛過十字路口，你一定要：

1. 停車，讓行人有優先權，然後小心前進
2. 停車，當交通安全才前進
3. 慢駛，交通安全才前進
4. 停車，直至燈號轉綠色，同時安全才前進

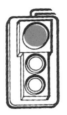

4

53. If you are involved in a reportable accident how soon must you make a report to your nearest provincial or municipal police officer?

1. At once
2. Within 24 hours
3. Within 48 hours
4. Within 72 hours

53. 如果你置身在一件交通意外，而一定要報警，在什麼時間內，你要報告給最近你的省警察或當地警察？

1. 立刻
2. 在二十四小時內
3. 在四十八小時內
4. 在七十二小時內

1

54. Upon approaching a stop sign, a driver must:

1. Slow down, sound horn and proceed
2. Slow down, and if the way is clear, proceed
3. Stop, sound horn, then proceed
4. Stop, and when it is safe to do so, proceed

54. 當你駛近“停牌”時，你應：

1. 慢駛，響號然後前進
2. 慢駛，當安全才繼續前進
3. 停車，響號然後前進
4. 停車，當安全才前進

4

55. You are required to keep a safe distance behind the vehicle in front of you at 50 kilometres (30 miles) an hour. You should keep at least:
1. Seven car lengths behind the other vehicle
2. Three car lengths behind the other vehicle
3. One car length behind the other vehicle
4. Five car lengths behind the other vehicle

55. 當你駕駛每小時50公里（30哩）應該和前面車輛最少保持多遠才安全：
1. 七個車位的距離
2. 三個車位的距離
3. 一個車位的距離
4. 五個車位的距離

`2`

56. A "school bus", with red signal lights flashing, stops on a highway that has no median strip. What does the law require you to do when meeting or overtaking the bus?
1. Does not matter provided you sound horn
2. Stop until the bus proceeds or the signal lights are no longer flashing
3. Wait for approaching vehicles to pass
4. Reduce speed and pass with care

56. 一輛"校車"閃紅燈停在中間沒有欄杆或障礙物的高速公路中，無論你是迎面而來或從後面超越，法律要求你：
1. 沒有關係，只要你響號
2. 停車，直至校車前進或紅燈已不再閃
3. 等待接近的車輛駛過
4. 減低速度，同時小心駛過

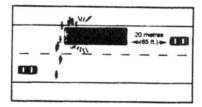

`2`

57. When the driver of another vehicle is about to overtake and pass your vehicle you must:
1. Move to the right and allow such vehicle to pass
2. Speed up so that passing is not necessary
3. Signal the other driver not to pass
4. Move to the left to prevent passing

57. 當你知道另一輛車準備駛過或超越時，你應：
1. 駛向路的右邊，讓他超越
2. 加速使他不能超越
3. 打燈號暗示他不要超越
4. 駛向左邊，阻止他超越

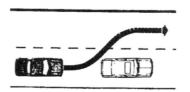

`1`

58. A G-licence driver may be required to attend an interview and re-examination of his driving ability:
1. When 9 demerit points have been accumulated
2. When 3 demerit points have been accumulated
3. When 6 demerit points have been accumulated
4. When 15 demerit points have been accumulated

58. G牌駕駛者可能需要被接見問話或重考駕駛技術：
1. 當駕駛過失而被記下的分數達到九點
2. 當駕駛過失而被記下的分數達到三點
3. 當駕駛過失而被記下的分數達到六點
4. 當駕駛過失而被記下的分數達到十五點

1

59. Should your right wheels drop off the roadway, what is the best way to get back on the roadway?
1. Steer hard to left
2. Apply brakes and steer hard to the left
3. Take foot off gas pedal, turn back when vehicle has slowed
4. Apply brakes to reduce speed

59. 當你右邊車胎駛入路邊泥地，那一個是最好的方法讓汽車駛回路面？
1. 大力把方向盤扭去左邊
2. 踏腳掣並大力把方向盤扭去左邊
3. 腳離開油門，讓車輛慢下來時才駛回路面
4. 踏腳掣以減慢速度

3

60. When approaching an intersection and you notice the roadway beyond the intersection is blocked with traffic, you should:
1. Keep as close as possible to the car ahead
2. Proceed slowly into the intersection until the traffic ahead moves on
3. Stop before entering the intersection and wait until traffic ahead moves on
4. Sound horn to warn cars ahead to move on

60. 當你接近十字路口時，發覺十字路口前面交通很擠迫，你應：
1. 貼著前面的車輛行駛
2. 慢慢駛入十字路口，直至前面交通暢通後才前進
3. 停在十字路口之前，等待前面交通暢通後才前進
4. 響號警告前面車輛前進

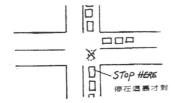

3

61. When a streetcar stops to pick up or discharge passengers and there is a safety island, what does the law require you to do?
1. Pass with caution
2. Stop at least 2 meters behind the safety island
3. Sound horn and pass with caution
4. Pass on the left side of the streetcar

61. 當電車停站讓乘客上落，當時是有一個安全島，在法律上你應怎樣做？
1. 小心駛過
2. 停在安全島後最少2公尺
3. 響號小心駛過
4. 在電車的左面駛過

1

62. Most automobile skids are the result of:
1. Under-inflated tires
2. Over-inflated tires
3. Snow or ice on the road
4. Driving too fast

62. 大多數汽車滑胎的原因是：
1. 車胎氣不夠
2. 車胎太多氣
3. 路上有雪或冰
4. 駕駛速度太快

4

63. What must a driver do before entering a highway from a private road or driveway?
1. Sound horn and proceed with caution
2. Enter or cross the highway as quickly as possible
3. Give hand signal then take right-of-way
4. Yield right-of-way to all vehicles approaching on the highway

63. 由私家路駛入公路之前，駕駛者應：
1. 響號並小心前進
2. 盡快駛入或橫過公路
3. 打手勢及取優先權先行
4. 讓所有駛近公路的車輛有優先權

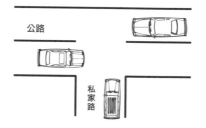

4

64. Parking lights may be used:
1. At any time
2. For parking only
3. When driving in heavy fog
4. When driving on well lighted street

64. 在什麼時候可用泊車燈？
1. 什麼時候都可以
2. 在泊車時用
3. 在大霧中駕駛時用
4. 在光線充足的街道上駕駛時用

2

65. If you are driving and suddenly one of your tires blows out, you should:
1. Concentrate on steering
2. Take your foot off the gas pedal to slow down
3. Bring the vehicle to a stop off the road
4. All of the above

65. 當駕駛時你其中一個車胎突然爆胎，你應：
1. 集中注意在方向盤
2. 腳離開油門使車速減慢
3. 使汽車停下在路旁
4. 以上全部都是

4

66. How close to a fire hydrant may you legally park?
1. 3 meters (10 ft.)
2. 4.5 meters (15 ft.)
3. 1.5 meters (5 ft.)
4. 6 meters (20 ft.)

66. 法律規定泊車距離救火喉多遠才是合法的：
1. 3公尺(10呎)
2. 4.5公尺(15呎)
3. 1.5公尺(5呎)
4. 6公尺(20呎)

1

67. As a level two (G2) driver your alcohol level must not be over:

1. 0.08%
2. 0.05%
3. 0.02%
4. 0.00%

67. 如果你是第二階段駕駛者，你要維持酒精量不超過：

1. 百分之0.08
2. 百分之0.05
3. 百分之0.02
4. 百分之零

`4`

68. When you are deciding whether or not to make a "U" turn, your first consideration should be to check:

1. Traffic regulations
2. Presence of trees, fire hydrants, or poles near the curb
3. Turning radius of your car
4. Height of curb

68. 當你決定"U轉"與否之前，你首先應查看：

1. 交通規則
2. 有沒有樹、救火喉或路邊燈柱
3. 你的汽車轉彎的範圍內
4. 路邊的高度

`1`

69. Why is it necessary to check over your shoulder when changing lanes?

1. It is a good exercise for your neck
2. There will always be a blind spot in your mirrors, no matter how you adjust them
3. To see who is driving
4. All of the above

69. 為甚麼在換線時要查看盲點？

1. 這個運動是對你的頸部好
2. 無論怎樣調校，你的鏡子總有些盲點的
3. 要看看誰是駕駛者
4. 以上全部都是

`2`

70. A solid centre line on the roadway is on your side of a broken centre line. What does the solid centre line mean?

1. It is unsafe to overtake and pass
2. Pass only when no traffic is in sight
3. It is safe to overtake and pass
4. Pass at any time

70. 路的中間，有一實線，有一虛線，而你靠近實線，實線的意思是：

1. 扒頭或超越是不安全的
2. 沒有車輛時才可以超越
3. 扒頭及超越是安全的
4. 隨時都可以超越

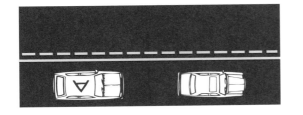

1

71. You must report an accident to the police under what condition?

1. There is less than $600 damage
2. The damage is over $1000
3. If someone has been hurt or killed
4. 2 and 3 are correct

71. 你如發生交通意外，在甚麼情況下一定要報警？

1. 損失少過六百元
2. 損失超過一千元
3. 如有人受傷或死亡
4. 以上 2 及 3 都是對的

4

72. Except when you intend to overtake and pass another vehicle or when you intend to make a left turn, you should:

1. Drive in the centre of the roadway
2. Always keep well to the right
3. Drive on the shoulder of the highway
4. Always keep well to the left

72. 除非你打算扒過及超越另一車輛，或想轉左，否則你應：

1. 駕駛在路的中間
2. 時時靠路的右面行駛
3. 在公路的路肩上行駛
4. 時時靠路的左邊行駛

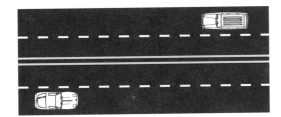

2

73. If you are convicted of drinking and driving, you will lose your driver's licence on the first offence for:

1. 1 month
2. 3 months
3. 6 months
4. 1 year

73. 如果你被控醉酒行車，第一次會被罰停牌多久？

1. 一個月
2. 三個月
3. 六個月
4. 一年

4

74. Level one and level two drivers must have a blood alcohol level of zero when driving. New drivers caught drinking and driving will be charged under the Criminal Code and will get how many days suspension?

1. 30 days
2. 60 days
3. 90 days
4. 1 year

74. 第一階段及第二階段駕駛者，在駕駛時體內酒精量是零，如果被捉到，除刑事法外還要停牌多久？

1. 30天
2. 60天
3. 90天
4. 1年

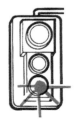

30 Days

1

75. A flashing green light at an intersection, where turns to the left and right are permitted, means:

1. You may turn to the left if the way is clear
2. You may turn to the right if the way is clear
3. You may proceed straight through if the way is clear
4. You may do any of the above

75. 在十字路口，轉左及轉右都准許時，綠色閃燈表示：

1. 路上安全，你可轉左
2. 路上安全，你可轉右
3. 路上安全，你可直駛
4. 你可做以上任何的

4

76. If you are driving and your cellular phone rings, what should you do?

1. Pick up the phone quickly and talk briefly while driving
2. Let your voice mail service take the call and check your messages when you are parked
3. Answer your phone if there are no police around
4. Turn-off, it is illegal to talk on the cellular while driving

76. 如果你在駕駛時手提電話響，你應怎樣做？

1. 在駕駛中盡快簡短地談話
2. 用電話留言，當車停下時再查口信
3. 如果鄰近沒有警察就可以談話
4. 駕駛時是不准用手提電話的

`2`

77. If a traffic signal changes while a pedestrian is still in the street, which of the following has the right-of-way?

1. Motorists making turns
2. The pedestrian
3. Motorists coming from his right
4. Motorists coming from his left

77. 如果交通燈轉了，而行人仍然在過馬路，以下誰有優先權？

1. 駕駛者正在轉彎
2. 行人
3. 駕駛者從右面駛來
4. 駕駛者從左面駛來

`2`

78. Highway 407 is:

1. The longest highway in Ontario
2. Is a new highway
3. Is an express toll route (paid toll highway)
4. An expressway to the USA

78. 407高速公路是：

1. 安省最長公路
2. 是一條新公路
3. 是一條快速收費公路
4. 快速公路通去美國

`3`

79. Except when passing, what distance must be maintained between commercial vehicles travelling in the same direction on the highway outside a city, town or village?

1. 30 m (100 ft.)
2. 60 m (200 ft.)
3. 120 m (400 ft.)
4. 150 m (500 ft.)

79. 在離開城市、鎮或鄉村的高速公路同一方向行駛，除超越外，跟在商業汽車後面應保持什麼距離？

1. 30公尺（100呎）
2. 60公尺（200呎）
3. 120公尺（400呎）
4. 150公尺（500呎）

60公尺

2

80. To what penalties is a driver liable who is convicted of driving while disqualified?

1. A fine of $500 or imprisonment for six months or both
2. Impoundment of the motor vehicle being operated for three months
3. An additional 6-month period of suspension of driving privilege
4. Any or all of the above

80. 駕駛者被停牌，而被控再次駕駛，他應受什麼責罰？

1. 罰款五百元、或入獄六個月、或兩樣都罰
2. 將汽車扣留三個月
3. 再加多六個月不准駕駛的權利
4. 以上任何一點或全部

4

81. A flashing blue light mounted on a motor vehicle indicates:

1. A motor vehicle carrying explosives
2. Snow removal equipment
3. An ambulance
4. A police emergency vehicle

81. 在車上裝有籃色閃燈是表示：

1. 車內載有爆炸品
2. 鏟雪的車輛
3. 救傷車
4. 有緊急事的警車

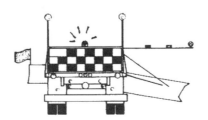

2

82. **When approaching a railway crossing at which an electrical or mechanical signal device is warning of the approach of a train, you must:**

1. Stop not less than 1.5 m (5 ft.) from the nearest rail
2. Increase speed and cross tracks as quickly as possible
3. Stop not less than 5 m (15 ft.) from the nearest rail
4. Slow down and proceed with caution

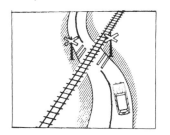

82. **當駛近火車路時，看到有電動式的機械訊號或有人拿旗號警告有火車來時，你應：**

1. 停車在距離路軌最少1.5公尺（5呎）
2. 加速盡快駛過火車路
3. 停車在距離路軌最少5公尺（15呎）
4. 慢駛，小心前進

3

83. **If you are involved in an accident in which someone is injured you must:**

1. Report the accident at once to the nearest provincial or municipal police officer
2. Report the accident within 48 hours to the nearest provincial or municipal police officer
3. Report the accident to your insurance company only
4. Report the accident to the Ministry of Transportation and Communications only

83. **如果你置身於交通意外，而當時有人受傷，你一定要：**

1. 立即與最接近的省警察或當地警察報告意外
2. 在四十八小時內報告意外與最近的省警察或當地警察
3. 只要向你的保險公司報告意外
4. 只要向交通部報告意外

1

84. **Under which of the following conditions is it dangerous and unlawful to make a "U" turn?**

1. Upon a curve or on a hill where there is a clear view of less than 150 m (500 ft.) in either direction
2. On a railway crossing or within 30 m (100 ft.) of a railway crossing
3. Within 150 m (500 ft.) of a bridge, viaduct or tunnel if driver's view is obstructed
4. Under all of the above conditions

84. **以下什麼情形下"U"轉是危險和不合法的?**

1. 在彎路或在斜坡，視力從兩方向150公尺（500呎）內看不清楚時
2. 在火車路上或火車路30公尺（100呎）內
3. 在橋、高架公路或隧道中150公尺（500呎）內，視力受阻礙時
4. 以上所有的情形都包括在內

4

85. Demerit points lost will remain on your driver's record for a period of _____ , from the date of offence:
1. One year
2. Two years
3. Three years
4. Five years

85. 由定罪那天起，過失點停留在你駕駛記錄多久：
1. 1年
2. 2年
3. 3年
4. 5年

2 Years

2

86. Before moving your car from a parked position, you should:
1. Check other traffic, signal and pull from curb quickly
2. Honk your horn and pull from curb slowly
3. Check other traffic, signal and pull from curb when it is safe to do so
4. Signal and pull from curb

86. 當你把車駛出停車位前，你應：
1. 看交通情形，打燈號及立刻駛離路邊
2. 響號然後慢慢從路邊駛出
3. 看清楚交通情形，打燈號，當安全的時候才從路邊駛出
4. 打燈號，然後駛出路邊

3

87. If you are approaching an intersection and the traffic lights are not working, you should:
1. Yield to the traffic to your right
2. Stop until no cars are passing and then go
3. Treat it as a four way stop sign
4. Slow down and proceed with caution

87. 如果你駛近十字路口而交通燈壞了，你應：
1. 讓右面交通先行
2. 停，直到無車時才駛過
3. 處理如四面停牌一樣
4. 減慢小心地駛過

3

88. When descending a steep hill a good safe-driving practice is to:

1. Gear down and use motor to assist in braking
2. Turn off the ignition
3. Place the gear shift in neutral
4. Disengage the clutch and coast

88. 當汽車駛下斜坡時，最安全的 方法是：

1. 用低波行駛及利用機器幫助煞掣
2. 扭熄汽車機器
3. 用中波行駛
4. 解脫汽車離合器，使車溜下

1

89. Failing to stop for a school bus that is unloading passengers will:

1. Result in a one year jail sentence
2. Cost you 6 demerit points and a fine of up to $1000
3. Get you a warning and a fine of $100
4. Result in retaking your road test

89. 當校巴停下上落乘客，而你駛過會怎樣：

1. 監禁一年
2. 扣六分及罰款高達一千元
3. 警告及罰款一百元
4. 重考路試

2

90. Unless otherwise posted, the maximum speed limit on the highway outside of a city, town, village or built-up area is:

1. 100 kilometres (60 miles) an hour
2. 80 kilometres (50 miles) an hour
3. 60 kilometres (40 miles) an hour
4. 50 kilometres (30 miles) an hour

90. 除非有特別標誌，否則在城市、鎮、鄉村或發展區以外的公路，最高的駕駛速度是：

1. 每小時100公里（60哩）
2. 每小時80公里（50哩）
3. 每小時60公里（40哩）
4. 每小時50公里（30哩）

2

91. **Which of the following hand-and-arm signals is correct for slowing or stopping?**
    1. Arm out and up
    2. Arm straight out the window
    3. Arm out and down
    4. Circle motion

91. **以下那一種手勢訊號是表示慢駛或停車?**
    1. 手臂伸出向上
    2. 手臂伸直向窗外
    3. 手臂伸出向下
    4. 轉圓圈的動作

3

92. **If your brakes fail:**
    1. Pump the brake pedal
    2. Apply the parking brake gently but firmly
    3. Keep your hand on the release button (of the parking brake)
    4. All of the above

92. **如果你的腳掣失控:**
    1. 在腳掣上用一踏一放方法
    2. 逐漸地拉緊手掣
    3. 手按著手掣的按鈕上
    4. 以上全部都是

4

93. **When driving a motor vehicle on the highway at night, you should use low beam headlights (dim lights) when:**
    1. Approaching an intersection
    2. Meeting or following another vehicle
    3. Another driver dims his lights
    4. Blinded by the headlights of an approaching vehicle

93. **夜間在快速公路行駛時,你必須用低燈,當你:**
    1. 接近十字路口
    2. 遇到迎面有車來或跟別的車輛時
    3. 當其他車輛用低燈
    4. 遇到迎面車輛的車頭燈,使你看不清楚

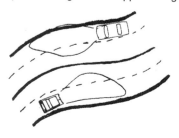

2

94. Level one drivers (G1) must keep their blood alcohol level at zero percent and be accompanied by a class G driver with a blood alcohol level of less than:

1. 0.00%
2. 0.05%
3. 0.08%
4. 0.03%

94. 第一階段駕駛者，你一定不准喝酒駕駛，而陪同的G牌乘客酒精要少過?

1. 零度酒精
2. 百分之0.05
3. 百分之0.08
4. 百分之0.03

`2`

95. It is more dangerous to drive at the maximum speed limit at night than during day-time because:

1. Some drivers unlawfully drive with parking lights only
2. You cannot see as far ahead at night
3. The roadway are more apt to be slippery at night
4. Your reaction time is slower at night

95. 在夜間以最高限制速度行駛比日間更危險，因為：

1. 一些非法駕駛者只用泊車燈行駛
2. 在夜間，你不能看得前面很遠
3. 在夜間，路面更容易濕滑
4. 你的反應在夜間會較慢

`2`

96. As a level one or level two driver you will have your licence suspended if you collect 9 or more demerit points during a two year period. 60 days after suspension your record will be reduced to:

1. 6 points
2. 4 points
3. Zero
4. 2 points

96. 在兩年內第一階段及第二階段的駕駛者，過失點在9分或以上時，在停牌60天後過失點減到：

1. 6分
2. 4分
3. 0分
4. 2分

4 Points

`2`

97. If you are a teenage driver aged 19 or under, in the first six months after receiving your G2 licence, how many teenage passengers are you allowed to carry between midnight to 5 a.m.?

1. 3 passengers aged 19 or under
2. No passengers aged 19 or under
3. 1 passenger aged 19 or under
4. 2 passengers aged 19 or under

97. 如果你是青年駕駛者，剛在六個月內考取G2牌照，在深夜12時到早上5時，你可乘載多少個青年乘客？

1. 3個在19歲或以下的乘客
2. 不准有乘客在19歲或以下
3. 1個在19歲或以下的乘客
4. 2個在19歲或以下的乘客

*（青年駕駛者是指未滿20歲者）

3

98. If you are a teenaged driver, after six months with your G2 licence and until you obtain your full G licence or turn 20, how many teenage passengers are you allowed to carry between midnight to 5 a.m.?

1. 3 passengers aged 19 or under
2. No passengers aged 19 or under
3. 1 passenger aged 19 or under
4. 2 passengers aged 19 or under

98. 如果你是青年駕駛者，考取G2牌照超過六個月後，在沒有考得G牌或還未滿20歲時，你可以在深夜12時到早上5時乘載幾多少個青年乘客？

1. 3個在19歲或以下的乘客
2. 不准有乘客在19歲或以下
3. 1個在19歲或以下的乘客
4. 2個在19歲或以下的乘客

1

99. There are some exemptions for a teenaged G2 driver, if you are accompanied by a fully licensed driver with at least _____ years of driving experience in the front seat or if your young passengers are members of your immediate family? (Midnight to 5 a.m.)

1. 2 Years
2. 3 Years
3. 4 Years
4. 5 Years

99. 青年駕駛者有些例外，如果有一個_____年G牌駕駛者坐在前排或其他青年乘客都是他直屬家人。（在12 a.m. 至 5 a.m.）

1. 2年
2. 3年
3. 4年
4. 5年

4 Years

3

ANSWER 答案

100. The broken centre line on a roadway means you may:

1. Never pass
2. Pass if the way is clear
3. Pass at any time
4. Pass only during daylight hours

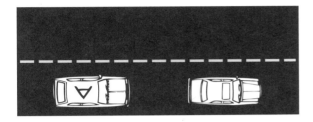

100. 路的中間有虛線是代表：

1. 不准超越
2. 可以超越，當交通安全時
3. 隨時可超越
4. 在日間才可以超越

2

101. If you are involved in an accident that was due to your use of a cellular phone while driving:

1. Your insurance will increase
2. You will be charged with careless driving and lose 6 demerit points
3. Your license will be suspended for one year
4. You will have to take your road test again

101. 如果你駕駛時因使用手提電話發生意外：

1. 你的保險費增加
2. 你會被控訴危險駕駛及扣六分
3. 你要停牌一年
4. 你要重考路試

2

102. At night when you meet another vehicle with blinding bright lights, the safest thing to do is:

1. Open and shut your eyes rapidly
2. Look at the headlights of the approaching vehicle
3. Turn your high beam lights on
4. Look slightly to the right hand side

102. 在夜間行駛，當你遇到迎面車輛車燈很強烈耀眼，使你看不清楚，最安全的方法是：

1. 迅速的將眼睛一開一合
2. 看迎面車輛的車頭燈
3. 把車燈轉用高燈
4. 把視線稍微望向路的右手邊

4

駕駛常識

Knowledge for all Drivers

103. At 15 demerit points, your licence is suspended, after 30 days, the number of points on the driver's record is:

1. Reduced to 7 points
2. Reduced to 0 point
3. Reduced to 5 points
4. None of the above

103. 當過失點達到十五分，牌照要吊銷三十天後，在恢復駕駛時的分數，將會：

1. 減到七分
2. 減到零分
3. 減到五分
4. 以上全部都不是

7 Points

1

104. When 15 or more demerit points have accumulated on a record, the driver's licence is suspended:

1. Automatically, and for 30 days from receipt of licence
2. At the discretion of the Ministry
3. Only if the licence is NOT used for business purposes
4. For 3 months

104. 當駕駛者的過失紀錄達到十五點或以上時，執照將受暫停：

1. 自動停牌，從退回執照給交通部起停牌三十天
2. 由交通部再審查
3. 如執照不是作商業用途
4. 三個月

30 Days

1

105. The Ministry of Transportation and Communications may suspend a licence after a 9 demerit point interview:

1. If a driver fails to give satisfactory reasons why their licence should not be suspended
2. If a driver does not have at least 5 years driving experience
3. If the licence is not needed for business reasons
4. The Ministry is not permitted to suspend a licence before the 15-point level is reached

105. 當駕駛過失達到九點時，被接見問話後，交通部可能暫停駕駛者執照：

1. 當駕駛者不能提出充份的理由反對停用執照
2. 當駕駛者沒有五年的駕駛經驗
3. 如駕駛者的執照不是作商業用途
4. 駕駛過失除非達到十五點，交通部是不能暫停執照的

1

安省駕駛執照制度
ONTARIO CLASSIFIED DRIVER LICENSING SYSTEM

等級	准許駕駛的車輛		亦准駕駛
A	Any tractor-trailer combination	大型貨車	D and G
B	Any school purposes bus	大型學校巴士	C, D, E, F and G
C	Any regular bus	公共巴士	D, F and G
D	Any truck or combination provided the towed vehicle is not over 4,600 kg 貨車或被拖的車箱不超過4,600公斤以上		G
E	School purposes bus—maximum of 24 passenger capacity 小型學校巴士不超過二十四個乘客		F and G
F	Regular bus—maximum of 24 passenger capacity—and ambulances 不超過二十四個乘客的車輛或救傷車		G
G	Any car, van or small truck or combination of vehicle and towed vehicle up to 11,000 kg provided the towed vehicle is not over 4,600 kg 全車牌——任何私家車，小型貨車或車及拖箱車共重不超過11,000公斤，而拖車不超過4,600公斤		
G1	*Level One of graduated licensing*—Holders may drive Class G vehicles when accompanied by a fully licensed driver with at least four years of driving experience. Additional conditions apply 第一期學車紙		Replaces Class L Licence
G2	*Level Two of graduated licensing*—Holders may drive Class G vehicles without accompanying driver but are subject to certain conditions 第二期准車牌		Replaces Probationary Status
M	Motorcycles—Holders may also drive a Class G vehicle under the conditions that apply to a Class G1 licence holder	電單車牌（摩托車牌）	
M1	*Level One of graduated licensing*—Holders may drive a motorcycle under certain conditions 第一期學電單車紙		Replaces Class R Licence
M2	*Level Two of graduated licensing*—Holders may drive a motorcycle but only with a zero blood alcohol level. Holder may also drive a Class G vehicle under the conditions that apply to a Class G1 licence holder 第二期准電單車牌		Replaces Probationary Status

第二部份: 路試 (Road Test)

駕駛不小心,禍害你一生。
學車學錯師,一生後悔遲。
為何開始錯,如今選擇時。
由於學鐘少,車禍才至知。

你覺得這本書對你考筆試及路試有幫助嗎?
歡迎各位讀者電郵我們,分享你的的經驗或難題

budgetpublishing@hotmail.com

沒有新知識,不會有進步;
沒有盡其力,不會有改進。

編者
梁成基
TOM LEUNG

自動波

Automatic Transmissions

P — PARK 停車（泊好車後，波桿要放在 P 才可離開汽車）

R — REVERSE 退後（車輛後退時用）

N — NEUTRAL 空波（車壞了，需要人推到路邊，洗車或拖車時用）

D — DRIVE 前進

3 —
LOW 低波（上山或下山時用或減慢汽車速度）
2 —

1. 自動波汽車，通常有三種速度，也有些兩種或四種，當放在 D 前進時，自動波自會產生效力，駕駛者減少一切煩惱

2. 從 P 到 R 或轉 D 一定要腳踏煞車掣，汽車要完全停下才可轉檔否則汽車機件很容易壞，而且危險

3. 方向盤（Steering Wheel）——— 控制兩個前輪的擺動

4. 煞車掣（Brake）——— 腳踏下時，用來減慢速度或停車

5. 手掣（Parking Brake）——— 停車時用來鎖著後輪胎（停在斜坡時更需要用）

6. 油門（Accelerator or Gas Pedal）——— 控制汽車速度

交叉手正確方法

Hand Over Hand Steering

在北美洲交叉手是正宗而最佳的手法，手法正確可幫助駕駛者轉彎準確及靈活。

正確停車位置

Correct Stopping Positions

停牌 STOP SIGN

當駕駛者遇著這個路牌時，無論在甚麼情形下，一定要把車完全停下，看清楚各方面絕對安全才可行。

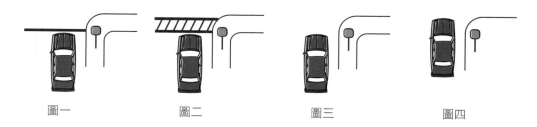

圖一　　　　　圖二　　　　　圖三　　　　　圖四

圖一：馬路上有粗白線時，停車在粗白線的後面

圖二：停在班馬線的後面

圖三：停在行人路之後

圖四：如無白線、班馬線或行人路，正確停車位置是在路的末端，車頭和路邊看齊

圖五：四面停牌 —— 十字路口四面都有停牌，則先停者有權先行（如兩部車同時到達，則右方車有優先權）

圖六：三面停牌 —— 在三叉路口及三個停牌的馬路，先停車者有優先行（如兩部車同時到達，右方車有權先行）

圖七：ALL WAY —— 先停先去

圖五　　圖六

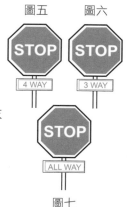

圖七

盲點及換線方法

Blind Spots and Lane Changes

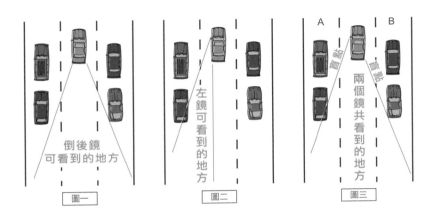

左鏡可看到的地方

兩個鏡共看到的地方

倒後鏡可看到的地方

盲點

圖一　　圖二　　圖三

在日常駕駛中換線佔很重要的地位，不安全換線常引起車禍，圖三所示 A 及 B 部份是盲點，即兩鏡都看不見的位置，因此換線前一定要回頭快捷地看一看盲點（Blind Spot Check）。

【 換進A線方法 】	【 換進B線方法 】
1. 打左燈	1. 打右燈
2. 看倒後鏡	2. 看倒後鏡
3. 看左鏡	3. 快捷回頭望向右 B 面盲點角
4. 快捷回頭望向左 A 面盲點角	4. 安全才駛入 B 線
5. 安全才駛入 A 線	

⚠️ 注意：
* 在每小時行50公里（km），車速最少二秒鐘跟車距離（三個車位）
* 在天氣不佳、大貨車、巴士後面，最少三秒鐘跟車距離（四、五個車位）
* 在高速公路每小時100公里，最少四、五秒跟車距離（七、八個車位）

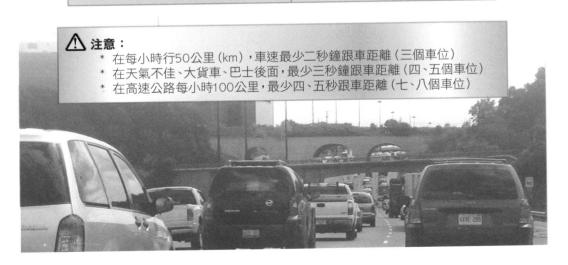

馬路行車線

Pavement Lane Markings

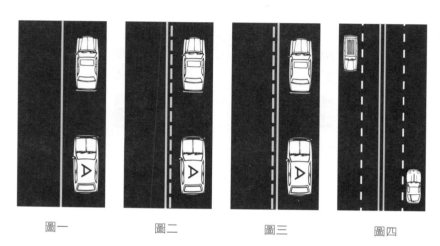

圖一　　　　　　圖二　　　　　　圖三　　　　　　圖四

圖一：黃色實線 ── 在左邊表示不安全超越

圖二：黃色虛線 ── 表示A車可以超越，當前後交通安全的時候

圖三：黃色實線 ── A車不應該超越

圖四：白色虛線是分開同一方向交通行車線。黃色實線是分開兩方不同方向的交通

兩邊轉左線：如下圖

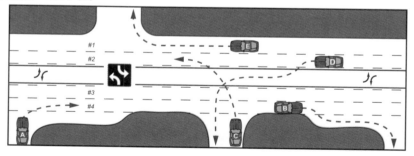

　A 車從橫街轉出如有巴士停車處不應駛入

　B 車從大街入橫街如有巴士停車處應從巴士站駛入

　C 車從橫街左轉出大街，不用駛入兩邊轉左線

　D 車從大街入橫街，左轉前一定要先駛入兩邊轉左線

　E 車即普通右轉

保持兩秒鐘跟車距離方法

Two Second Rule

保持安全的距離，是駕駛者不能忽略，同時很重要的，很多時我們用車位代表車與車之間的距離。新方法用時間計算與前面車子的距離更為有效，這種行車方法能讓駕駛者有足夠的位置去應付前面突然變化的交通，同時讓視線的角度增加，有足夠的時間隨時煞車，時刻有良好的駕駛習慣，使行車較輕鬆和安全，避免意外或引致死亡發生。

兩秒鐘行車距離方法 Two Second Rule

圖一　　　　　　　　圖二　　　　　　　　圖三

圖一：　在公路上，前面的車輛將到達一路牌

圖二：　當前面的車輛車尾剛過路牌時作為起點，開始數一千零一

我們數一千零一、一千零二（One thousand and one, one thousand and two）。這兩句說話大概等於兩秒鐘，我們的車頭還未超過起點的路牌，即我們有一個安全的距離

圖三：　相反的，如果還未數到一千零二，我們的汽車已超過起點，即我們與前面車輛有危險的距離

以下的情況下更應保持安全的距離：

1. 跟著大貨車、大巴士或電車後面
2. 駛近十字路口、交叉點、交通燈、班馬線或火車路等
3. 在彎路、轉角、路面修窄時
4. 路旁很多泊車、學校地帶及市區行人擠迫處
5. 當後面車輛跟車太貼，尤其是在高速公路上
6. 看不清楚前面交通情況：如大霧、路滑、猛烈陽光、大雪、大雨等

日間與夜間駕駛

Day and Night Time Driving

1. 陽光猛烈時，帶適合的太陽眼鏡，避免望向太陽中心點，利用汽車的「擋陽光板」（Sunvisor）

2. 白天，從路面駛入隧道，或地底停車場出路面，切要慢駛，讓眼睛漸漸適應

3. 日夜間駕駛都要保持玻璃清潔，有足夠的視覺

4. 晚間駕駛發生意外較高，因眼睛只看到日間的百分之七十五，速度應稍為減慢

5. 遇著迎面車輛開高燈，應把視力望向路旁

6. 身為一個安全駕駛者，時刻留心突然閃出的行人，腳踏車，同時小心孩童、小動物從車的兩旁走出

7. 在駕駛時視野不清，如大霧、下雨、大風雪、在日落前半小時、在日出後半小時或任何時間150公尺（500呎）內看不清楚事物時，一定要把車頭燈開著

左轉及右轉的重點

How to Make Left and Right Turns

左轉 LEFT TURNS

1. 首先觀察左轉是否安全、合法?
2. 遠望前面十字路口,盡早靠左線(包括看倒後鏡、左燈號、看盲點)
3. 把車駛到中間線的右邊
4. 減慢速度
5. 以左、中、右的方法,再看一次十字路口
6. 看清楚交通燈號及路牌標誌,讓路與有優先權的車輛及行人
7. 需要時再看左盲點
8. 安全下用交叉手方法,向著左面線轉去
9. 遠望,把方向盤回直,安全下加油直駛

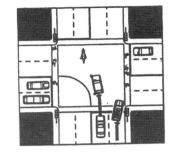

⚠️ **注意:** 當等候迎面的車輛通過時,盡量把車胎拉直。

右轉 RIGHT TURNS

1. 首先觀察右轉是否安全、合法?
2. 遠望前面十字路口,在安全下盡早靠右線(包括看倒後鏡、右燈號、看盲點)
3. 減慢速度
4. 以左、中、右的方法再看一次十字路口
5. 看清楚交通燈號及路牌標誌,讓路與有優先權的車輛及行人
6. 有必要時再看右盲點(如有腳踏車及路人)
7. 以交叉手方法右轉,保持與路邊距離約一公尺
8. 遠望,把方向盤回直,安全下加油直駛

⚠️ **注意:** 在安大略省紅燈右轉是合法的,但一定要在白線後完全停下來 (Complete Stop),當左面沒有來車及行人,在安全下才可右轉;但如看到紅燈不可右轉牌時 (No Right Turn on Red Sign),就要等到綠燈才可右轉。

三點式掉頭

Three Point Turn

在掉頭前首先要觀察：1. 是否合法
2. 是否安全

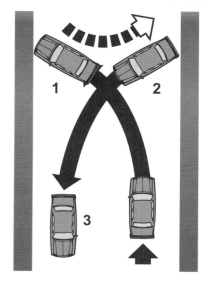

第一步

1. 先減慢速度，打右燈，靠最近右方路邊停下，使能充分利用馬路的闊度

2. 打左燈，望倒後鏡，同時轉頭向左看盲點，觀察安全後盡快把方向盤扭盡左方，慢慢前進

第二步

3. 小心停車，距離路邊約兩三呎

4. 打右燈入後波（Reverse Gear），確定四周環境安全，快速把方向盤扭盡右方，慢慢後退

第三步

5. 當車子後面接近行人的路邊時停定

6. 入前波（DRIVE），打左燈，向左右觀察，肯定安全下快速把方向盤扭盡左方，擺直車子，遠望直駛去

重要點：

1. 掉頭時小心慢駛
2. 轉方向盤手法要快捷，交叉手法最佳
3. 停車時小心煞車
4. 前進及倒後時，看清楚你所行駛的方向，行人及障礙物
5. 燈號是左、右、左

斜坡泊車方法

Parking on a Hill

1. 上斜坡泊車（有行人路邊）——— 將前胎扭盡左邊，拉緊手掣（圖一）

2. 下斜坡泊車（有行人路邊）——— 將前胎扭盡右邊，拉緊手掣（圖二）

3. 上斜坡泊車或落斜波泊車（無行人路或路邊）——— 將前胎扭盡右邊，拉緊手掣（圖三）

以上幾種斜坡泊車，只有（1）在上斜坡（有行人路邊）是將前胎扭盡左邊，其餘的方法都是扭向右邊，理由是當汽車失控擎時，避免汽車溜出馬路，阻礙交通及發生意外

⚠ **注意：** 做泊車時要看倒後鏡，打右燈，小心駛近路肩。

平行泊車

Parallel Parking

泊位，原則上車速應越慢越好，只有車速慢，才有充分的時間去判斷方向盤應該甚麼時間扭動，方向盤則應越快越好，多熟練，泊位就會泊得好。

平行泊車，即與路邊平行停泊，一般在繁忙市中心及多行人的街道上進行，更要停在兩輛車的中間，因此這是初學者最煩惱及有技巧的一課。

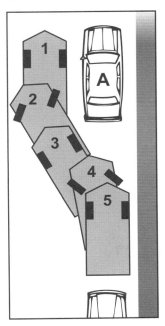

1. 選擇車位，留意交通，打右燈作泊車訊號，慢駛

2. 駛向車位，距離A車約兩呎，與A車平行，車尾和A車尾成一直線時停下

3. 看倒後鏡，轉後波（R波），同時留意四周及看左面盲點，交通安全後，轉方向盤向右方，慢慢退後

4. 直至車頭和A車尾成直線時立刻轉方向盤向左方，讓後輪近路邊時，把車開前擺正，保持前後一空間

5. 放在Park及拉手掣

⚠️ **注意：** 好的泊車是與路邊不應超過一呎，同時右邊前後輪不能碰路邊，駛車離開車位時要注意打燈，看鏡，轉頭向左方望盲點，待安全時才駛出馬路。

【泊車方法如圖，速度慢而安全，後退時頭要向後望，要多多練習。】

九十度角前後泊車法

90° Angle Parking

（一）退後泊車 BACK IN

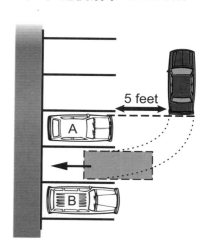

5 feet

第一步

1. 打左燈
2. 駛直自己的車與A車的左角成一直線停下，距離A車約5呎（一架車位）
3. 看倒後鏡及回頭望過四周
4. 安全下盡快把方向盤扭向左
5. 慢慢向著空位退入，直到與A、B車成直線

第二步

6. 把方向盤回直，眼看清楚四周，慢慢退後入
7. 如果感覺危險，可拉直駛前，左右關顧慢慢地控掣入空位中

⚠ **注意：** 後退時要向後望。

（二）前進泊車 DRIVE IN OR HEAD IN

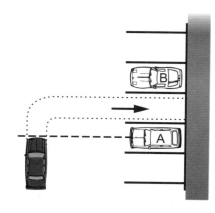

1. 觀察車位慢駛
2. 打右燈
3. 遠離A車7至8呎
4. 讓A車的右邊與自己車頭成直線
5. 以交叉手法盡快右轉
6. 慢駛，左右關顧，在與A車及B車之間回直方向盤
7. 速度應較慢而安全

⚠ **注意：** 泊車時車速慢，關注四周車輛及行人，停在合理位置。

史密夫駕駛方法

The Smith System

是北美最盛行的一種安全駕駛方法，由美國人史密夫先生(Harold Smith)首創，令駕駛者有安全的駕駛習慣，時刻清楚四周的交通情況，在意外發生前有所警覺，同時提防第三者的駕駛錯誤，其五點如下：

（一）駕駛時眼睛向遠望 Aim High in Steering

1. 眼睛遠望前面中心點，選擇安全的目標，手控制方向盤，自然駛向路線的中心
2. 保持遠望前面十二至十五秒行車距離的交通，通常在市區的駕駛速度，最少能看到前面整條街的交通環境，在高速公路的速度，則最少能看到前面三分之一哩的交通

（二）觀察前面交通環境的全面 Get the Big Picture

1. 保持視野看得廣闊一點，鍛鍊自己觀察四周、路的左右，時刻留意兩邊行人路和馬路末端
2. 視察停泊的車輛、行人、電燈桿、腳踏車、交通燈及行車線等
3. 時刻與前面和左右車輛保持安全的距離
4. 速度隨著路牌和交通情況而增減
5. 眼睛不要集中在任何一點而忽略其他

（三）眼望四方 Keep Your Eyes Moving

1. 保持四周空間位置(Space Cushion)，跟著安全的距離行駛
2. 在特殊及不安全的環境下減低速度駕駛，例如天氣惡劣：大霧、下雪、視野不清、下雨路滑、行人多、上山下山及窄路等
3. 避免跟車太近，選擇最安全路線行車
4. 讓自己能夠有清楚而無阻的視線，不宜跟巴士、大貨車太近，或停留在盲點太久
5. 時常提高警覺，尤其是隱藏的道路、山丘、彎曲小路等

（四）避免陷入危險的境界 Leave Yourself An"Out"

1. 保持每兩秒鐘或以上跟車距離，常轉移視線，不要定神望向一方
2. 快速以"左中右"的過程視察十字路口，留意車輛突然打開車門及準備開出
3. 習慣每五至八秒鐘望倒後鏡一次

（五）肯定他人看到你 Make Sure They See You

1. 眼睛與眼睛聯繫(Eye-Contact)，盡快讓行人和別的駕駛者知道你的動向，大家以眼睛表示，意外自然可避免或減少
2. 訊號表示(Communications and Signals)，和前後車輛及行人有聯繫，利用響號、燈號、手勢及眼神等

交通燈號

綠燈：Green Light

表示可以直駛、左轉及右轉，在左轉時要讓迎面駛來的車子及面對綠燈的行人，右轉時要讓綠燈行人。注意直駛，如在交通密集及綠燈時，汽車不准擠塞在路口中。

閃綠燈：Advance Green Light

表示有優先權左轉、直駛及右轉，在閃綠燈時迎面車及其他方向車輛及行人都是面對紅燈。閃綠燈時間短，很快變回綠燈。

黃燈：Yellow or Amber Light

表示紅燈即將出現，如果你可以安全停下就必須停車，倘若不能安全停下便小心前進。

一盞閃黃燈：Flashing Yellow

表示小心駛過，但要觀察左右。

一盞閃紅燈：Flashing Red Light

表示首先停車，如面對停車牌一樣，要完全停下，在安全時才可前進。

紅燈綠箭咀：Red Light with Green Arrow

表示你可以從左轉行車線內左轉。（對方燈號也是一樣或紅燈）

紅燈黃色箭咀：Red Light with Yellow Arrow

從綠色的左轉箭咀變黃色，指兩個方向的車流快將出現綠燈，最好停下車輛，如果不能安全停下，要盡快小心左轉。

紅燈：Red Light

表示必要將車子停下（停在白線或行人路後面）等待綠燈。在安大略省，紅燈可以右轉，但先要完全停下，讓路給優先權左面來的車輛及行人才可右轉。（單程路轉單程路時，紅燈也可以左轉，停定，安全下才可左轉）

閃紅燈：Flashing Red Light

表示燈號不能正常運作或壞了，如見到停牌一樣，先停定，在安全下才可駛過。（如果交通燈完全壞了，作為四面停牌，先停先走）

單程路

單程路即是只有一個方向行車的道路

如何分辨是單程路?

1. 路中間沒有黃色分界線
2. 街道的出入口兩邊都放有箭咀
3. 停泊在馬路兩邊的車輛,車頭都是向著同一方向
4. 街道的出口盡頭,有「不准駛入」路牌
5. 單程路通常有兩個停牌,一左一右
6. 行駛馬路時兩面的路牌及標誌都清楚看見
7. 左手面車輛都與你同一方向行駛

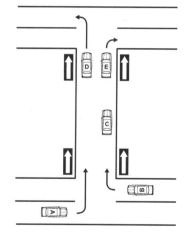

入單程路的駕駛方法:

1. A 車從雙程路左轉入單程路要駛入單程路的左面
2. B 車從雙程路轉右,要駛入單程路的右方
3. C 車在單程路駕駛要駛在右手面馬路上(左面是超越線用)
4. D 車從單程到雙程路,首先把 D 車駛到單程路的左面,安全下左轉
5. E 車從單程路轉右,靠右,安全後,才駛入雙程路

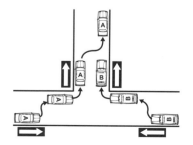

單程路轉入單程路的行駛方法:

1. A 車左轉入單程路
2. B 車右轉入單程路

⚠ **注意:** 安省規例,單程路入單程路紅燈可以左轉,先靠車在左面,停車,看清楚行人及交通安全下才轉。

什麼是防禦駕駛?

Defensive Driving

防禦駕駛也是安全駕駛,駕駛者預先警覺路上隨時有可能發生的意外,用適當的駕駛技術去脫險及防衛自己和車輛。要成為一個安全、防禦駕駛者,你應明白及服從所有交通規則,同時感應路上、天氣和交通的轉變,為了自己和車上各人的安全,必定扣上安全帶,行車時與前面相隔一段安全的距離,如兩秒距離的方法 (Two Second Rule Driving),遇著突然危險和緊急的情形時,給自己有「逃生」的路線,而不會手忙腳亂,如果面臨撞車而不能逃避的情形下,盡量駛去安全的方向,避免碰頭撞,如碰頭也不能避免,把車輛方向稍為傾斜。時刻集中精神駕駛,避免使用手提電話,留意及警覺別人不安全駕駛,大半以上的交通意外都是由於駕駛者的大意和不留神而發生。

以下六個位置和情形時刻警戒

(一) 留意前面的車輛:

1.　停在路邊的車輛,留意車內的人突然打開車門或打燈駛出
2.　前面車輛突然慢駛或停車
3.　前面車輛會在斜坡倒後嗎?

(二) 後面的車輛,利用倒後鏡去看:

1.　後面車輛跟車太貼,你停車會安全嗎?
2.　如後面的車輛跟車太近,你應慢駛,讓後面的車輛超越或駛向路旁一邊,讓他先行

(三) 迎面的車輛:

1.　那車輛會駛過中線嗎?
2.　在晚間行駛,駕駛者是否開高燈
3.　留意對方是否不集中精神駕駛或醉酒行車

（四）在左右兩邊行駛的車輛：

1. 留意駕駛者會不會不停「停牌」
2. 沒有看清楚而駛出十字路口、私家路口、巷等
3. 有沒有減低速度讓路給優先權者
4. 對方用敵視眼光看著你時，如發怒、激烈、瘋狂、不禮貌、無理取鬧等，切不可直視或理論，有機會時寫下他們的車牌號碼

（五）汽車被他人超越時，應留意：

1. 左右車輛突然超越，駛入你車頭前面
2. 留心左面或右面準備超越的車輛，減慢速度和觀察後面車輛的距離

（六）汽車準備超越前：

1. 超越是否安全？
2. 有沒有足夠的空位和迎面而來的車輛速度？
3. 有沒有打正確的燈號？
4. 是否看清楚「盲點」？

彎角 Curve

當你車趨近彎角，盡早決定安全車速。最好跟隨交通標誌速度，這些標誌顯示安全速度。當你車距離彎角還有三十公尺之時，你需已經減速至安全車速。在一些看不到前路的彎角，你更需慢駛，避免與前面來車相撞。在開始進入彎角之前就需慢駛，避免在彎角內煞車。在彎角駕駛時，要盡可能看到四周情況。這可以幫助你選取一條暢順的行車線，在轉彎時最好不要換行車線。

 注意：在晚間、雨天、大霧及冰雨天入彎時更要小心。

高速公路駕駛方法

Expressway Driving

高速公路通常指兩條以上向著同一方向的快行車線,同時有指定的出口和入口,速度通常在八十至一百公里以上,故駕駛者必須小心謹慎、正確判斷、反應靈活。當遇到特殊危險大風雪、晚間駕駛、大霧、大雷雨等都是在高速公路常見發生意外的原因。在多數的高速公路為安全起見,行人及腳踏車是不准行走,長的高速公路更是省過省的。由於公路快速,不能停車或慢駛,最好上高速公路之前先翻閱一下地圖,假如你錯過了一條出口,切勿後退而應繼續前進,看清標誌從下一出口轉回。

駛入高速公路重點及方法 Entering Expressway

1. 速度要標準,在入公路前聽清楚考官告訴你的方向,如 Don Valley Parkway North(即向北面),401 East(即東面)等。

2. 在進入高速公路變速彎(RAMP)時,要觀察前後車輛跟車安全距離,如四十公里,切不能超速。在天氣不佳時,可能減至三十公里不等,切勿跨越白色線。

3. 在加速線上要打正確燈號,加速到公路上的速度,提高判斷力,特別注意在公路上行駛車輛的速度及行車線位置,看清楚交通情況,看倒後鏡,看盲點,在安全下從加速線盡頭平穩地加入車流中。(見圖一)

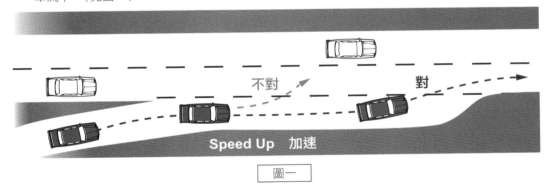

不對　對

Speed Up　加速

圖一

高速公路駕駛方法 Driving Along in Expressway

1. 眼睛遠望安全目標,雙手控制方向盤,視野在十五至二十秒以外,不停觀察,用左、右、左的視線警界著兩邊車輛危險。

2. 每五至八秒望倒後鏡一次,跟車有三至四秒安全距離,換線時要打正確燈號、看盲點,不宜跟大貨車及巴士太近或停留盲點太久。

3. 時常靠右線行駛,最左線是超越線,在考試中考官會考驗考生高速換線技術,留心路牌。

4. 在天氣惡劣、視野不清、交通擠塞時,要多多忍耐減慢車速,但在正常交通的高速公路,不能減慢,要時常保持一百公里時速行駛才比較安全。

駛離高速公路 Exiting Expressway

1. 先檢查交通情況，在駛進出口線(Exit Lane)之前，看左看右觀察，並看倒後鏡觀察後面的交通，看清楚那一條是安全出口線，打正確燈號，看盲點。

2. 從減速出口線的開端處進入，保持平穩車速，直到你的車完全進入出口線後才可減慢。

3. 小心回旋處彎角(RAMP)標誌速度牌，若果有兩條出口線，不可跨越地面實線，要保持與前面車有安全距離，小心合併路。

4. 在離開高速公路時要小心方向、市內速度、路人、燈號等。（初學者最好在不繁忙時間多多練習）

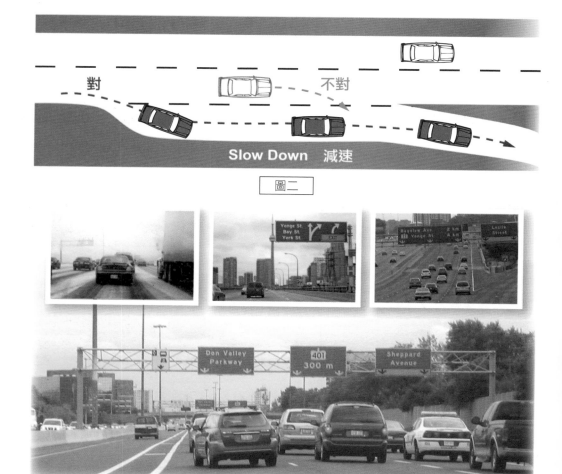

對　　　　　　　不對

Slow Down 減速

圖二

路邊停車

檢查交通情況

在慢下來停車之前，看倒後鏡檢查後面的交通情況，若右邊車輛或行人超越你的話，你需看清楚右邊盲點之後，才可以靠近路邊停車。

訊號燈

在慢駛靠右近路邊停車前，勿忘打右邊訊號燈。

車速

當你駛近右邊停車時，需逐漸減速，不要急速停車。

停車位置

停車位置需與行人路肩保持平行，距離不要超過三十厘米或一呎。若果沒有高起的行人路肩，則盡量近路旁。停車時不要阻塞居屋的出入口處，或阻塞其他交通。關掉訊號燈，然後開啟車的四角泊車閃燈(4 Way Flashing)，把波棍放在 P 泊車檔，拉起手掣，關掉汽車引擎，此時腳可以離開腳掣。

路邊開車

開動引擎，把波檔放在 D (Drive)，鬆開手掣，準備返回路面。

訊號燈

關掉車的四角泊車閃燈，然後打左燈，檢查交通情況，開動汽車之前，看倒後鏡檢查車後的交通情況，並且看左盲點，在安全下才可駛出。

車速

平穩加速至正常車速，然後融入車流中，當你的車已經回到路面時，盡快關掉訊號燈。

駕駛小常識：停車距離

1. 校巴車頂閃紅燈時停在20公尺前後
2. 火車路如有火車來應停距離最少5公尺後
3. 電車有乘客上落應停在後門2公尺後
4. 泊車距離在救火喉3公尺前後
5. 在斑馬線前30公尺不得超越其他車輛

汽車意外應如何處理

An Accident

交通意外，在大多市可説是常見的事，例如駕駛者技術水準低、交通常識不足、精神不集中、沒有讓優先權、天氣欠佳、風暴、冰雨、大雪道路濕滑、追隨前面車輛太近、沒有一個安全距離、汽車機件失靈、速度太快等等，都會引起汽車意外，嚴重的引致人命慘劇，小的汽車受到損壞。安大略省新例，雙方估計意外不超過一千元而無人受傷，可自行解決。

意外處理方法——不管有沒有人受傷，都面臨法律上的責任，可能受法律上控訴，為了保障自己，一定要知道當時環境，如果處理得好，當然會減少日後不必要的煩惱。

1. 立即停車，關閉油門，等警察來才可移動汽車(凡有關車輛發生意外時不停留在現場者，警方以犯刑事法處理)

2. 保持頭腦冷靜，記錄下對方汽車的車牌、顏色、年份和牌子

3. 請對方出示駕駛證，登記司機姓名、地址、執照號碼、電話、乘客姓名及人數、燕梳公司名稱及電話、燕梳號碼等

4. 如有人受傷，立刻叫路人幫助打電話報警或召喚救傷車、醫生

5. 記下發生意外汽車所去的方向，車速及損壞情形，用簡圖幫助記憶，如有相機，影下現場作日後記錄，切勿與對方爭執

6. 記下目擊交通意外自願證人姓名、地址及電話

7. 巡視意外地點，查看附近各處有沒有交通燈、交通標誌、地下煞車痕跡

8. 當時的天氣及路面情況，如下雪、大雨、冰雨、修路、交通擠迫

9. 記下調查失事警察的姓名、編號、警局、電話等。日後如有問題可以直接與他聯絡

10. 記下傷者的姓名、醫院名稱、地址、電話等

11. 馬上通知自己律師和保險公司，並詳細説出當時發生失事的經過

12. 打電話叫拖車或駛去車廠修理

13. 如在快速公路上發生意外，就要立刻把車駛離公路，停在安全的地方，避免引起更多意外事件，直至警察人員到達為止

14. 如有傷者受傷，以毛氈或外衣墊於傷者保暖，以乾淨的布條或潔淨的毛巾及用壓點方法制止其流血，立刻找醫生或明白急救人仕幫手

15. 如在郊區發生意外，找不到警察，要在廿四小時內到最近的警局或省警察報案

16. 在多倫多市，當繁忙的時候，如沒有人受傷或沒有嚴重車禍，在電話報案後要自行駛車到鄰近的報案中心報案(地址如後)

多倫多市
交通意外
報案中心

Collision
Reporting
Centres

緊急電話號碼
9-1-1

非緊急電話號碼
(416)808-2222

北區報案中心

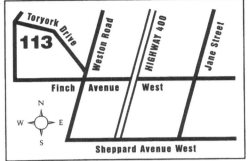

113 Toryork Dr. 電話號碼：(416) 745-1600

士嘉堡報案中心

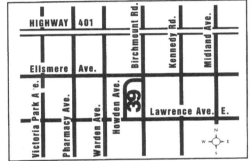

39 Howden Rd. 電話號碼：(416) 701-1600

西區報案中心

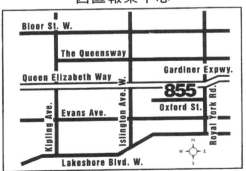

855 Oxford St. 電話號碼：(416) 252-1200

烈治文山區： 9350 Yonge St. (Hillcrest Mall) 電話號碼：(905) 881-1221
密西沙加區： 4600 Dixie Rd. 電話號碼：(905) 453-3311 ext. 1200
3030 Erin Mills Parkway 電話號碼：(905) 453-3311 ext. 1100

冬天駕駛須知

Preparing For Winter Driving

在加拿大每一年有很多新移民及年青新牌者加入冬天駕駛行列，由於缺乏新環境及雪地經驗，很容易會發生交通意外，在冬天嚴寒的天氣和時刻風雪，隨時變幻無常的駕駛環境，駕駛者要加倍跟車距離及作以下的準備，便會減少意外發生。

（一）汽車在冬天前準備

1. **汽車檢查及調整（Tune-up）**

   冬季來臨之前，應徹底調整汽車機件，宜採用輕份量多種性能的機油，例如應用 5W/30，太濃和重機油，使機器行駛吃力。時常檢查冷凝液（Car's Coolant），應每兩年更換新液一次。

2. **換雪胎（Snow Tires）**

   冬季前預早換上雪胎，預防不測的天氣，滑輪（Skid）是交通意外的主要因素。

3. **電池（Battery）**

   電池一定要保持良好狀況，舊和弱的電池使冬天打火更困難，保持電池端及鉛的部份清潔和乾爽，加些少潤滑膏在電池端能防止腐蝕及較耐用，通常好的電池可用四至五年。

4. **預備工具**

   隨車帶備雪鏟、玻璃窗雪掃（Ice Scraper）、防凝液、手套、毛毯、電筒、傳電線（Jumper Cables）等，住在冬天天氣特別冷的地方，應存沙包、沙土，在冰雪上可增加汽車摩擦力。

5. **後窗除霜器**

   一定要安置和保持良好情況，前面水撥如果舊了必要換新，時常保存洗窗液（Windshield Washer）-40°C，清潔窗口，記著有好的視線才能避免意外的發生。

（二）開車之前的準備

1. 首先清潔所有窗、車頭、車頂和車燈的冰雪。

2. 盡快開車，好幾分鐘便可以，最初幾分鐘不要加速太快，是節省汽油的最好方法，其步驟因車而異，應參考你的汽車手冊。

如車尾滑向右邊，把方向盤轉向右邊
（看 P.24 #27）

（三）滑胎 Skidding

1. 如果汽車滑向一方，首先要鎮定，千萬不可踩煞車掣，只要將汽車前輪轉向車尾滑去的同一方向，汽車就可以重新受控制，當回復完全控制下小心煞車或直駛。（下雪天可在無人無車的停車場練習）

2. 雪地慢駛或停車 —— 把腳離開油門，切勿太急煞車，不然汽車會滑向一方。煞車時，保持均勻的力度，使汽車直線停下或一踏一放的方法，如果你轉彎時大力煞車，會令前輪鎖死，令汽車滑向一側。

3. 與前面的車輛保持一段安全的距離，如果汽車滑輪胎時，也能安全停車，避免與前面車輛相撞。

4. 具有 ABS（Anti-Lock Brake System）煞車系統則煞車時須一次踩到底，系統會幫助自動煞車，詳細請看車主手冊。

（四）陷於雪中 When Stuck in the Snow

如果被困於雪中，加強警覺，依照下列去做：

1. 用鏟將車輛四周的雪鏟去（車廂應常備鏟子）。

2. 在車胎下放舊地氈，留意前胎一定要擺直，然後用低檔前進。

3. 如果沒有氈子，可加一些沙石或鹽在輪胎下，使車輪增加摩擦力。

4. 搖擺車輛，以產生動力，如果車是自動波，轉波時要踩煞車掣，如不停的轉前波又後波，會傷汽車的傳動系統（TRANSMISSION）。

5. 慢慢開動，避免車輪空旋，令輪胎下的雪壓成冰。

6. 若果真的陷於雪中，盡量發出求救訊號，例如發出警告訊號燈、在天線及車門上縛一條現眼的布條或用手提電話報警。

壞的車

好的電池

（五）困於風雪：假如被困於風雪，而不安全繼續行駛，應：

1. 留在車中，每隔一小時打引擎十分鐘，籍以保暖和充電池。
2. 時常開些少窗，保持空氣流通。
3. 留意廢氣喉沒有被雪掩蓋，不然死氣會入汽車內。

（六）其他提示：

1. 在特別冷的地方，使用局部電暖器(Block Heater)容易打火。
2. 若駛過半溶的雪或水潭，煞車系統入了水，使煞車掣失靈，須輕輕的踏煞車掣，因摩擦熱量逐漸蒸發水分，煞車掣便會回復正常。
3. 遇著長途旅行，或荒僻的路途，預算較長的時間，並預先告訴親友所到的地方和抵達的時間，帶備少許乾糧及手提電話等。

怎樣考路試成功？

除選擇一間優良的駕駛學校，有耐心、經驗豐富的好師傅，價錢是決定師傅經驗及學校質素，更要加倍用功，不要節省堂費而日後增加保險費及重考費用，緊記正確方法，熟能生巧，失敗乃成功之母。考路試時，考牌官會考驗學車者的駕駛經驗如：(a)開車 (b)停車 (c)左轉右轉 (d)交通路牌及燈號 (e)超越換線 (f)十字路口 (g)平行泊車及退後駛 (h)道路上的指示線 (i)斜坡停車 (j)安全駕駛(沒有危險動作) (k)窄路掉頭 (l)駕駛的反應及觀察。

考車牌決不單是考駕駛技術，最重要是安全駕駛，留心考牌官的指示，保持鎮定，集中精神，同時留意行人、路牌、速度、交通情況及火車路等。考驗完畢，考牌者即可知道合格與否，合格後立即發給臨時車牌，即可駕駛。

東區考試場貼士

東區考試場
Lawrence Centre

地址：1448 Lawrence Ave. East (Victoria Park Ave.)
辦公時間： 8:30am - 5:00pm

⚠ **注意**：如考生不在這試場應考，其他考試場的要求也是大同小異，以下可作參考

試場要特別留意事項：

1. 東區試場附近是工業及住宅區，在 Lawrence Ave. 及 Victoria Park Ave. 是60公里，Pharmacy Ave., 及 Curlew Dr. 是50公里，住宅區內40公里，有些急彎街道減至30公里。

2. 試場位於大商場內，在開始及出入停車場內駕駛要小心行人及停泊車輛，速度不要太快(約15至20公里)，聽清楚考牌官指示。

3. 試場路面高低不平，大路車輛比較多，小路有急彎，故小心車速不要太快或太慢。

4. 在十字路口閃綠燈，表示可以左轉、直去及右轉；單一盞閃紅燈表示要把車完全停下，左右安全時才駛過。

5. 在跟著巴士或大貨車後面，切勿跟得太近，保持一個安全距離，除非是壞車或特慢車輛，最好不要超越爬頭，要注意四周交通。

6. 要小心學校巴士，在九時前及下午三時後都有校巴在區內行駛，如見車頂閃紅燈，前後交通都要停駛，讓路給學童橫過(停在20公尺後)。

7. 常靠右線行駛，左線是超越線，如果有三條行車線，也要靠最右線駕駛，除非考官叫你不用換線。

8. 停牌：考生必定要把車子完全停下，停的位置要標準，如看不清楚左右交通必要流前再看，安全下才通過。四面停牌就是先停先去。

9. 在平行泊車及上下斜坡泊車做完後，在考生駛車離開前要注意看鏡、打燈號、望盲點才可駛出。

10. 如聽到救傷車、警車及救火車響號，考生要看清楚它們從那方來，安全立刻把車駛向右邊停駛，讓路通過。

11. 東區考場沒有單程路及火車路，但要注意優先權，轉彎時要小心行人，紅燈右轉一定要完全停在白線前看清楚行人及左面來的車輛才可右轉。

12. 東區考場，考試路線範圍在 Lawrence Ave. E., Victoria Park Ave., Pharmacy Ave., Curlew Dr., Lynvalley Cres., Surrey Ave., Sloane Ave., Carnforth Rd. 一帶考驗。包括：（1）三點式掉頭（2）平行泊車（3）安全駛駛考驗（4）紅綠燈左右轉（5）內街駛駛考驗（6）斜坡泊車（7）換線、觀察力及優先權（8）回來時用九十度角前或後泊車。

13.

巴士線：A車轉出如有巴士停車處不應駛入　B車轉右如有巴士停車處應駛入（如圖）

14. 留心考牌官的指示，保持鎮定，集中精神，同時留意行人、路牌、速度、交通情況、優先權等，如果聽不清楚考牌官的指示可再問，在沒有緊急事故切不可突然停車，引起後面危險，在下雨天及雪地上車速可以減慢，但切勿太慢。

右轉　　　　　左轉　　　　慢下或停車

東區考路試場地圖

Lawrence East Centre

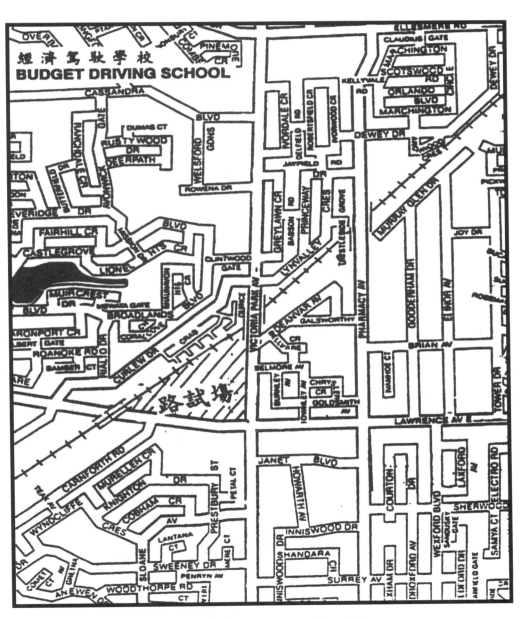

1448 Lawrence Ave East

汽車保養

Car Care

定期檢查及保養可增長汽車壽命，節省不必要的修理費，新出廠的汽車，最先8,000公里（500哩）內，行車速度每小時不應超過88公里（55哩），在最先320公里（200哩）內避免大力急停煞車，對煞車系統有損壞。

汽車保養分三部份

（一）每兩星期檢查

1. 洗窗噴水液（Windshield Washing Fluid）
2. 洗車（Car Wash）
3. 各類車燈（All Lights）
4. 引擎潤滑油（四年以上車齡）
5. 車胎及車胎氣壓（Tire Pressure）

（二）每二個月檢查

1. 電池（Battery）
2. 水撥（Windshield Wipers）
3. 水箱液（Anti-Freeze Fluid）
4. 煞車液（Brake Fluid）
5. 風油呔液（Power Steering Fluid）
6. 傳動系統液（Transmission Fluid）
7. 避震系統（Suspension System）
8. 廢氣喉（Exhaust System）
9. 發電機皮帶（Electrical Belt）
10. 水管及皮帶（Hoses & Belts）

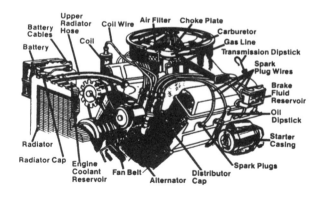

（三）以里數定期檢查：

1. 煞車掣 Brakes —— 每34,000 km或一年一次（煞車時有雜聲）

2. 摩擦潤滑液 Oil Change —— 每6,000 – 8,000公里。夏天用10W30，冬天用5W30油

3. 水箱 Cooling System —— 每兩年換新液一次（Anti-Freeze Fluid）

4. 前輪軸心 Front End —— 每12,000 km及Alignment車輪較對（當車行駛時常走向一邊或不能駛直線）

5. 空氣清潔器 Air Filter —— 18,000 km

6. 傳動系統液 Transmission Fluid —— 每49,000 km換油液及隔濾器一次

7. 車胎轉換 Tire Rotation —— 每10,000 – 12,500公里轉換，使車胎耐用百分之二十

8. 電池 Battery —— 每年清潔外面，在4至5年換新電池

每間車廠各有不同，詳細情形參閱新車手冊

車胎保養及轉換法 Tire Rotation

要保養好車胎，應每12,500公里（8,000哩）轉換一次，可使車胎耐用百分之二十

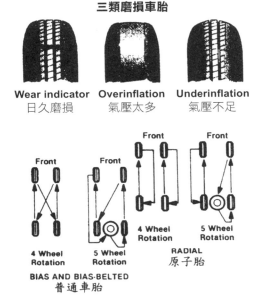

三類磨損車胎

Wear indicator 日久磨損　**Overinflation** 氣壓太多　**Underinflation** 氣壓不足

Front　Front　Front　Front

4 Wheel Rotation　**5 Wheel Rotation**　**4 Wheel Rotation**　**5 Wheel Rotation**

BIAS AND BIAS-BELTED 普通車胎　**RADIAL** 原子胎

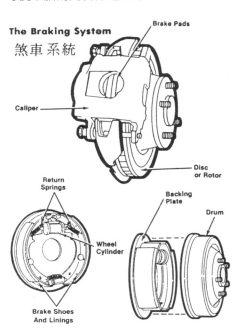

The Braking System 煞車系統

Brake Pads

Caliper

Disc or Rotor

Return Springs

Backing Plate

Drum

Wheel Cylinder

Brake Shoes And Linings

廿十點節省汽油的方法

20 Tips For Gas Saving

1. 選擇較少和輕便的車，越大和重的車輛，汽油消耗越多

2. 買四個汽缸的汽車比六個及八個的省油

3. 不需要時關上冷氣

4. 汽車的外型影響風速，買流線型的汽車最好，在開車時關上窗門

5. 用棍波的車輛及油渣車比自動車省油

6. 買前輪推動的車比後輪車及四輪推動車省油

7. 買原子車胎 (Radial Tire) 是最省油的車胎，而洩氣車胎加重氣油的負擔，要跟胎廠指定氣壓作標準

8. 用較好的機器潤滑油 (Motor Oil)，冬天宜用輕份量及多種性能的機油，例如 5W30，夏天10W30

9. 例行定期檢查汽車 (Tune up)，有良好的火花塞 (Spark Plugs) 常換新的空氣清潔器 (Air-Filter) 都可節省汽油

10. 雪胎比普通車胎浪費汽油百分之七以上，過了下雪的季節宜立即換回夏季車胎

11. 盡量減輕汽車不必要的重量，清除車廂內不需要的雜物

12. 投資新電動車 (Hybrid car)

13. 保持平穩的速度行駛，避免不必要的加油及煞車

14. 當停車時，無謂的開著汽車等於浪費汽油及產生廢氣

15. 每次入油時，要把所有汽油最後一滴入乾。看見加油車在油站進行保充汽油時，地底油箱內沉澱物加上新的汽油混雜，請勿加油，因太污穢汽油對發動機不好

16. 在特別寒冷天氣的地方，使用局部電暖器 (Block Heater)

17. 計劃每次路途，避免不必要的停站，用最短的路程到達

18. 每次入油時，記錄下價目及里數，以作比對每月支出

19. 油箱太滿增加汽車重量，應保持三分之二滿的汽缸

20. 留意價錢平和好的電油站，不要等到無油時入貴油

購買新車舊車須知

Tips for Buying New or Used Cars

在買車前，應再三慎重考慮，不應過急進行，千萬不要買經濟能力不及的高價車，須知買車後不僅要支出每月的供車費，還有每年牌照費、汽車保險、每月的汽油費、修理汽車費、泊車費用等。

購買新車

選擇可靠有信譽的車行，考慮到汽車的費用、安全設施、是否節省汽油等，購買新車的好處是新車通常有保用，也可以選擇自己喜好顏色，如果發覺機件有失靈，車行有保障，節省一筆修理費，更有些車廠提供加長保修保險、終身換機油及路邊援助服務。須知新車落地，價錢就即時折舊，因此需格外留意自己認為滿意的車輛。

購買舊車

買二手車可以説是很冒險事，因你不知道上手車主怎樣保養，是否曾經有車禍，最好找一個專業技師檢查，試車是很重要的。

1. 查看舊車的年份、牌子、保養、價錢是否公道。
2. 在白天仔細檢驗汽車，不要被名牌、外型所迷惑，查看汽車各機件使用情況如：煞掣、油門、車身的狀況等，堅持要試車，行車時留意車子是否偏向一方，行駛時有無明顯聲響，能否控制自如，最安全便是去熟悉的汽車修理廠檢查一下及聽取專業人事意見。
3. 核對車子的里程表(Odometer)，查看里數和車子的機件使用情況是否符合。
4. 在轉手前應向政府部門查明車主及車輛是否已付清費用。
5. 在成交六天內帶同安全標準檢驗證書、保險證、交零售税、領取新車牌。

無論買新車或舊車，簽合約前，要細心閱讀清楚列明所買的汽車、保養內容、舊車補錢換新車及整個交易詳述。如要貸款買車，車行應在合約上列明利息及利率、每次付款、及多少次還清。

安省交通法律規定，汽車必須買保險才能駕駛，同時駕駛機件不安全的汽車是違例的，汽車轉車主時一定要連同由車行發出的安全標準檢驗證書(Safety Standards Certificate)才能向登記署轉車主。1994年4月開始，每兩年要通過廢氣測驗(Drive Clean Test)，合格後才可換牌。

常見交通符號

Regulatory Signs

TRAFFIC SIGNS 交通符號

 停
 讓
 島右駛過
 前五十公里
 最高八十公里
 學校區
 不准危險物品
 不准貨車駛入
 超越線

 紅燈不准右轉
 不准左轉
 不准右轉
 只可左轉
 只可右轉
 不准轉
不准泊車
 不准停車
不准超越

 單程路
不准駛入
入錯方向
行人班馬線
三十分鐘停車
左或直去線
直去線
右或直去線
兩面左轉線

WARNING SIGNS 警告牌

 停牌在前
 讓牌在前
 紅綠燈在前
 火車路
 腳踏車過
 雪車橫過
 鹿橫過
 彎速度五十公里

 急彎
 合併路
 十字路口
 斜坡
 濕滑路
 高度不超過3.9米
 學校巴士轉彎
三十公里

 彎
 彎右
 彎曲路
 公路分叉
 窄路
 右線完
 凹凸路
 危險線

 慢行車輛
 修路在前
馬路完
公路修理
右面貨車出入
船過橋會升起
可能水掩路
石頭墜落

GUIDE SIGNS 指示牌

 電油站
 餐室
 酒店
 詢問處
 船可下水
 營地
 目的地

 醫院
 飛機場
 省公園
 省警察
公路牌
公路401
公路出口牌

路試常用英語

English For Road Test

1. Good morning Sir/Madam　早晨先生/女士
2. Good afternoon　午安
3. How are you?　你好嗎?
4. Do you speak English?　你講英語嗎?
5. I do not speak English　我不識講英語
6. I can speak a little English　我識很少英語
7. Please speak slowly　請慢慢講
8. Would you mind speaking louder please?　請説大聲些?
9. Do you wear glasses?　你有戴眼鏡嗎?
10. I wear contact lenses　我戴隱形眼鏡
11. Do you live at the same address?　你的地址沒有改嗎?
12. Do you have any medical problems?　你的健康有問題嗎?
13. Did you have a licence before?　你以前有車牌嗎?
14. Where did you get your driver's licence?　你在那裡考取車牌?
15. In Hong Kong, I've had it since 2003　在香港2003年已有車牌
16. Have you ever been suspended from driving?　你的車牌曾否被吊銷過?
17. You must obey all the rules and traffic signs　你要遵守所有交通規則及路牌
18. Do you have any questions?　你有什麼問題嗎?
19. Please sign your name here　請在這裡簽名
20. Are you ready now?　你可以開始嗎?
21. Turn on the engine (car)　打火，開引擎
22. Let's go　現在開始
23. Right turn　右轉
24. Left turn　左轉
25. Go straight/Keep going straight　直駛
26. First street right turn/left turn　第一條街右轉/左轉
27. Traffic light right turn/left turn　交通燈右轉/左轉
28. Stop sign, make a right turn/left turn　停牌右轉/左轉
29. Stay in this lane　保持在這條線行駛
30. Second street　第二條街
31. Turn on the headlights　開車頭燈
32. Turn on the windshield wiper　開水潑
33. Stop the car here　在這裡停車
34. Pull over to the curb　靠路邊停車
35. Slow down　慢駛
36. Three point turn　三點式轉(窄路掉頭)
37. Parallel parking　平行泊車

38. Uphill parking　上斜坡泊車

39. Downhill parking　下斜坡泊車

40. Back up　倒後退

41. Back into this driveway　倒後駛入這車路

42. Too close　駛得太近

43. Too slow　太慢

44. Too fast　太快

45. Speed up　加速行駛

46. Give a signal　打燈號

47. Cancel your signal　取消燈號

48. Try again　再做一次

49. Watch for pedestrians　小心行人

50. Take it easy/Relax please　請不要緊張

51. More gas　加油

52. Follow the car　跟著那車

53. Go back to the test centre　駛回考試場

54. Entrance　入口

55. Exit　出口

56. Right of way　優先權

57. Intersection　十字路口

58. Put on your seat belt　扣上安全帶

59. Turn on the heater/air conditioner　開暖氣/冷氣

60. Parking brake　手掣

61. Head in parking/Drive in　車頭入泊車

62. Road side stop　路邊停車

63. Highway 401 East　公路401 東面

64. Don Valley Parkway North　D.V.P. 北面

65. Lane change to the left and then go back to the right lane　先轉線到左線，然後轉回右線

66. Turn on your 4 way flasher　開著你的前後閃燈

67. Turn off your 4 way flasher　關了你的前後閃燈

68. Speed up to 100 km　加速到100公里

69. Turn off the engine　熄掉引擎

70. You have failed　你不合格

71. Do you have any identification?　你有什麼證件?

72. Try again later　下次再試

73. You have passed　你合格

74. Come with me　跟我來

駕駛過失點扣分表
The Point System Table of Offences

七點	發生交通意外不留現場而離開
六點	(1)不小心駕駛　　(3)比指定的時速超過五十公里或以上 (2)賽車　　　　　(4)沒有停車讓學校巴士
五點	巴士司機沒有在過火車路前停車
四點	(1)比指定時速超過三十公里及四十九公里內 (2)跟前面車輛太接近
三點	(1)比指定時速超過十六公里及二十九公里內 (2)在火車路欄桿下通過或繞火車路而駛 (3)沒有禮讓予有優先權者 (4)沒有遵守停牌、燈號或火車路訊號 (5)沒有遵守警察指揮 (6)沒有向警察報告意外事件及超越1,000元以上的損壞 (7)不安全超越 (8)駕駛者前列車位太擠迫 (9)入錯單程路或高速公路相反方向 (10)在關閉的高速公路行車 (11)使警察受傷害 (12)不合法使用特別高速快線及專用線
兩點	(1)未有用低燈行車　　　　　(7)沒有讓路 (2)不安全打開車門　　　　　(8)不合法右轉 (3)不合法的轉彎　　　　　　(9)不合法左轉 (4)利用汽車拖行腳踏車或雪車　(10)沒有打燈號 (5)沒有遵守路牌　　　　　　(11)不合理的慢駛 (6)不讓行人過斑馬線　　　　(12)在公路退後 (13)駕駛者沒有確保16歲以下乘客佩戴安全帶 (14)駕駛者沒有確保嬰兒安全及正確合法使用嬰兒座椅

G牌 ———— 達到扣九分時收到交通廳邀請問話，到十五分時停牌三十天，領回執照後紀錄減至七分，如兩年內再曾至十五分，停牌六個月。

G1及G2牌 ———— 達到扣六分時收到交通廳改善通知信，當扣至九分時，停牌六十天或停牌後重考（由執照交回交通廳之日計算，如拒絕交出執照停牌兩年）。停牌後紀錄減至四分，如兩年內再曾至九分，停牌六個月，如飲酒駕駛停牌三十天。

（所有駕駛者過失扣分紀錄檔案留存兩年）

1　　**2**　　**3**　　**4**　　**5**

6　　**9**

經濟出版社出版：

1. 最新筆試必讀　$7.50
   Driver's Handbook For Chinese Written Test

2. 最新考路試及高級手冊 (For G 牌)　$5.50
   Road Test and Advanced Driver's Handbook

3. 分級考牌制度，最新考筆試及路試手冊　$9.50
   Graduated Drivers' Handbook for Chinese Written Test and Road Test

4. 最新入籍指南 (Book 1)　$6.50
   How to Become a Canadian Citizen Book 1

5. 最新入籍筆試必讀 (Book 2)　$6.50
   The Canadian Citizen Book 2

6. 最新入籍筆試，問題及答案二百題 (Book 3)　$8.50
   The Canadian Citizen Written Test Book 3 (200 Questions and Answers)

7. 最新入籍指南 (粵或國語) 錄音帶　$6.75
   Cassette Tape & CD for How to Become a Canadian Citizen (Book 1)

8. 最新入籍筆試，問題及答案二百題 (Book 3) 錄音CD　$10.75
   CD for The Canadian Citizen Written Test Book 3 (200 Questions and Answers)

9. 最新公民入籍新知　$8.50
   Canadian Citizenship Study Guide (Book 4)

10. Just For You Driver's Handbook Study Guide—Knowledge and Road Test (English)　$13.95

10

(Sold in all Chinese Book Stores)

 If you would like to order additional copies, please send a cheque or money order of the cover price along with your name, address, and telephone number + $2.50 shipping and handling per book.

Payable to:　**Budget Driving School**
　　　　　　P.O. Box 32585, 9665 Bayview Ave.
　　　　　　Richmond Hill, Ontario L4C 0A2, Canada

如果需要買以上書籍，請寫支票付 "Budget Driving School" 寄來以上地址，
請清楚寫上你的姓名、地址、電話號碼 + 每本2.50元運費或各大唐人書局均有代售。